A Very Famous Social Worker

GREG JOHNSON

iUniverse, Inc.
Bloomington

A Very Famous Social Worker

iUniverse books may be ordered through booksellers or by contacting:

iUniverse
1663 Liberty Drive
Bloomington, IN 47403
www.iuniverse.com
1-800-Authors (1-800-288-4677)

Because of the dynamic nature of the Internet, any Web addresses or links contained in this book may have changed since publication and may no longer be valid. The views expressed in this work are solely those of the author and do not necessarily reflect the views of the publisher, and the publisher hereby disclaims any responsibility for them.

Any people depicted in stock imagery provided by Thinkstock are models, and such images are being used for illustrative purposes only.

Certain stock imagery © Thinkstock.

ISBN: 978-1-4502-8548-3 (sc)
ISBN: 978-1-4502-8549-0 (ebook)

Printed in the United States of America

iUniverse rev. date: 1/13/2011

Cover design by Blackbird Studios/Mary Baldwin.
Author photo by Nick Johnson.

In memory of
Anne Blair Alderson
1921 – 2000

Contents

I'd unravel any riddle
For any indivi'dle
In trouble or in pain ...

- If I Only Had a Brain
Lyrics by E. Y. Harburg

Introduction

It happened in Yokohama, Japan, where I had taken a group of young professionals from West Virginia on a cultural exchange for Rotary International. We were meeting with a local dignitary, sipping green tea around a long conference table and exchanging pleasantries, when Mr. Ishiwata, the grandfatherly soul who was showing us around, decided to explain my occupation to our host. He leaned forward in his chair and addressed him in the rudimentary English he had acquired on a trip to the States.

"In Japan social workers very low," he said, scowling and pointing at the floor like they were cockroaches. He raised his finger to the ceiling and his rubbery, expressive face lit up. "In America social workers very high! Mr. Johnson important man! Very famous social worker!" He sat back and smiled, pleased that he'd managed to confer a little status on his guest.

The dignitary nodded solemnly as my young friends struggled to keep straight faces. Tea dribbled from their mouths. I knew I'd never hear the end of it. They still think it's clever to introduce me this way.

Despite the efforts of the National Association of Social Workers to dress the profession in its Sunday best, its hardworking members rarely achieve any fame. According to the U.S. Bureau of Labor Statistics 600,000 people are in this line of work, but they're a largely invisible corps, engaging in activities vague in the public mind.

Google "famous social workers" and you come up with a tiny handful of names from the distant past. Jane Addams, who won the Nobel Peace Prize in 1931. Frances Perkins, FDR's Secretary of Labor who drafted the first minimum wage laws and midwifed the Social Security system. Whitney Young, who captained Lyndon Johnson's War on Poverty. Bright stars in their own galaxies, but not exactly Elvis or Oprah.

I traveled the back roads of West Virginia for 25 years in the name of this little-known occupation, encountering all manner of comedy and tragedy. I've often wondered why, with so many interesting stories to tell, so few social workers tell them. Is confidentiality the stumbling block? It didn't stop Sigmund Freud from chronicling his patients' neuroses, or James Herriott from telling the world about the quirky Yorkshire farmers who sought his veterinary help. Circumstances can always be changed and identities protected. Preoccupation seems a more likely culprit. Would-be saviors can always find better things to do than pen their memoirs. Retired saviors are a different story.

The events in this book took place in my first year as a young social worker, in the 70's. Since those days the profession has changed and become more specialized. But the basic people-helping-people-with-everyday-issues model endures. Social workers inevitably encounter epic calamities and heart-rending tragedies, but what I remember best are the ironic, smile-inducing episodes. These are the stories I like to share.

Greg Johnson
Lewisburg, West Virginia

Chapter 1
Back to the Garden

Her name was Anne Blair Alderson, and she was the local answer to Mother Teresa. Unlike the real one she wasn't concerned that chain-smoking, mild profanity or a little after-hours bourbon would damage her case for sainthood. She was the founder of the Greenbrier Valley Mental Health Clinic, and founding mothers could write their own job descriptions.

It was April and I was sitting in her office on Church Street in Lewisburg, West Virginia. I was a month away from receiving my Master of Social Work degree, on my way back to West Virginia University from a bluegrass festival, when a nagging little voice whispered that it was time to stop rolling from one keg party to the next and start looking for gainful employment. I'd served an internship in this rural valley's northern reaches the previous fall and I liked this part of the state, so I decided to check out job possibilities.

I was still wearing the rumpled flannel shirt, dirty jeans and mud-caked hiking boots I'd worn to the festival. I looked more like a wino in search of a bottle than a professional in search of a job, so I devised a plan: I'd poke my head in some unsuspecting agency's door, ask if they had any openings, then follow up by phone. This strategy immediately failed at the Greenbrier Valley Mental Health Clinic, where the attractive, friendly receptionist insisted the director would love to meet me. I protested in vain as she ushered me inside and escorted me up the hallway.

An hour later I was still there. Anne Blair was fiftyish and Rubenesque, with a wedge of auburn hair and a paisley scarf draped over her capable shoulders. I liked her instinctively – she laughed at the right times and she didn't seem to be concerned about how I was dressed. She was treating me like an old friend. I was getting ready to push the job issue when there was an insistent knock on her door. "Come in," she called out, and a uniformed deputy sheriff entered. His grave expression suggested some urgent crisis.

"I've got Gertie outside," he announced. "She was standing in front of the post office, naked as a jaybird."

"Oh shit," Anne Blair reacted. She swiveled in her chair, eyeballed the cruiser parked in front of the building and issued a loud sigh. "All right, bring her in."

"I'm not bringing her in here buck naked," he refused.

"Oh, come on, Fred. You know she just wants to go back to the hospital."

"That's where she belongs," he opined. "She had traffic backed up for two blocks in front of the post office."

"You can't hospitalize someone for being a nuisance," she reminded him. "She's got to be dangerous to herself or others."

"You don't think running around naked in public is dangerous?"

"Yes, but she has to qualify technically. What's your gut feeling? Is she having a psychotic episode or is she faking it?"

"My gut feeling is that I'm about to wrap her in a blanket and leave her in your waiting room."

"Don't you dare!" She sprang from her chair like a jack-in-the-box and hastily gathered some papers. "I'll interview her in the car and fill out the petition. I'll have Jayne call the courthouse and set up the hearing."

I tried to imagine the legal proceeding. Would the defendant appear in the nude or would they drape her in a spare judicial robe? They were heading for the door when Anne Blair remembered I was there. She looked back and flagged me. "Come on, Greg. You might as well see what this business is all about."

On the positive side this suggested she was thinking about hiring me. On the negative, I was already having second thoughts about this "business". I'd imagined myself sitting in a comfortable office, conducting leisurely therapy sessions with articulate clients over mugs of steaming coffee. Our insight-filled conversations would be interrupted only when they reached for tissues to wipe away tears of remorse and gratitude. This vision quickly faded as we traipsed outside. I saw myself chasing naked senior citizens up Washington Street and wrestling them into Depends. Was this where six years of higher education had gotten me?

"Gertie's one of our chronics," she gave me the lowdown. "She lived at Weston State Hospital for 20 years, and then the courts decided people shouldn't live in hospitals. She has a little apartment over the Ben Franklin store. She can't hold a job, she can't manage her SSI money, she can't cook and she won't stay on her meds. She does outlandish things so we'll send her back to the hospital."

"Deinstitutionalization," I recognized the problem. A nationwide movement to return the mentally ill to their home communities was underway, but many of the people who were used to institutional life weren't having any part of it. They considered the hospital their home. Sidewalks and alleyways from coast to coast were filled with the sad results.

She rolled her eyes. "It wouldn't be so bad if they'd give us the money to look after these folks. We do what we can, but most of the time they have to fend for themselves."

"Sounds like Gertie's come up with her own solution."

"She knows how to play the system," she agreed. "She's crazy like a fox."

We reached the cruiser and I saw the center of all this commotion sitting in the back seat. Fox wasn't one of the words that immediately sprang to mind. Gertie was a fleshy mountain of sags, bags and wrinkles. "Hey, Miz Alderson," she waved a jiggly greeting.

"Hey yourself, Gertie," Anne Blair said wearily. "You look ridiculous."

"How 'bout a cigarette?"

She ignored this request and instead gave her a mental status exam, a series of simple questions designed to test her orientation to reality. Gertie's sly smile suggested that she knew the difference between the right answers and the ones that would win her another vacation at state expense. She told us she was Queen Elizabeth, we were in Mexico and the year was 5000 B.C.

"She's putting us on," Anne Blair whispered.

"No kidding," I whispered back.

She turned back to her client. "Gertie, for Pete's sake, put your clothes on."

Gertie ignored this request and the little pile of clothing on the seat beside her. "C'mon, Miz Alderson - I need a smoke."

Anne Blair glanced at the deputy. He shrugged.

She was reaching for her Salems when I had an inspiration. Ignoring the fact that I didn't even work there, I stepped up to the window. "Gertie, if you put on your underwear, we'll give you a cigarette," I bargained. It was a page right out of Behavior Mod 101, but what did we have to lose?

Gertie turned and regarded me skeptically. "Who are you?" she demanded.

"I'm Greg," I kept it simple.

"You heard the deal, Gertie," Anne Blair played along. "You can have a smoke if you put on your panties." She pulled a cigarette from her pack and waved it enticingly.

Gertie's eyes followed the cigarette; it was obvious she was a slave to nicotine. Broadcasting her displeasure with loud grumbles, grunts and sighs, she dug out her panties and put them on.

"You look much better now," Anne Blair stretched the point a few miles. She slid her reward through the window.

"I need a light," Gertie reminded her.

I moved to Part Two. "We'll give you a light when you put on your bra."

Gertie was used to being the manipulator. Being the manipulated didn't sit well with her, and she gave me the evil eye. She knew we had her. She found her bra and slipped it on. This didn't exactly transform her into Cinderella ready for the ball, but things were definitely moving in the right direction. Anne Blair lit the cigarette with a flourish and Gertie took a deep drag and settled back in the seat to enjoy her smoke.

The veterans turned to their rookie with appreciative smiles. I was basking in the glow of their admiration, feeling certain I'd just landed a job, when behind their backs I saw Gertie casually removing her bra. I sprang to the window. "Stop!" I begged, perhaps with a little too much desperation on my face. "Gertie, please don't do that!" We watched helplessly as Eve returned to the Garden.

"She's crazy, but she ain't stupid," the deputy offered his own diagnosis.

Gertie pointed an accusing finger at me. "He's the stupid one!" She threw back her head and cackled. Put in my place, I watched quietly from the sidelines as Anne Blair filled out the commitment petition and signed it. The deputy thanked her and climbed in his cruiser. Queen Elizabeth and her royal coachman pulled away and disappeared around the corner.

"What happens to her next?" I asked.

"She'll have a medical exam and a hearing. By this afternoon she'll be back at the hospital. In a couple of months we'll get a call saying she's being discharged and we'll be back at Square One." A series of class action lawsuits would prompt the state to come up with a better system for caring for their Gerties, but this was the 70's and community-based care for the mentally ill was more of a nice idea than a practical reality.

This little episode had left me hazy about the clinic's mission. "So is this mostly the kind of thing you do?" I inquired.

"No, we do a little bit of everything," she assured me. "I usually handle the chronics because I've known most of them since day one. We've all found our niches."

"I'm kind of looking for one myself," I reminded her. I'd had enough jobs to know that *boss* could be synonymous with *petty tyrant*. Anne Blair seemed more like a mentor, and it was already painfully obvious that I needed one. Besides, I was looking for an adventure and this quirky little clinic had adventure written all over it.

"When could you start?" she popped the magic question.

"I graduate May 8th. I can start on the 10th." While she pondered this, I decided an apology was in order. "I'm sorry for butting in," I said. "I shouldn't have been so eager to demonstrate my incompetence."

She put a reassuring arm around me. "We're a whole staff of incompetents, Greg. You'd fit right in. I just don't know if we can afford to add another person. We've only got enough to pay you until July. I don't know what we'd do after that."

"I'd really like to work here."

The wheels in her head were still turning. "Our new fiscal year starts in July. If we hire you now and list you as a continuing position, the state might not notice we've slipped an extra body in on them."

"So I might have a job for two months or I might have one for the rest of my life?"

"That's about the size of it."

"Sounds good to me," I signed on. I was still at the point where all my possessions fit comfortably in my Jeep. When you're young and mobile you can afford to operate on blind faith.

I didn't realize that Gertie had just given me a preview of my 25-year social work career. I was out to save the world, and I didn't even suspect that the world had no intention of cooperating with my plans.

Chapter 2
Consider the Lillys

My mother's family roots were buried deep in the white sand and red clay of Florida's panhandle. I'd grown up in South Florida, where high-rises were gobbling up the beaches, and tract developments, trailer parks, shopping malls and fast food joints were sprouting like weeds. Something deep in my soul longed to live in a place that wasn't being choked by this kind of progress. My parents were dismayed by my failure to bond with our homeland, but fortunately the day had passed when your elders could choose your place of residence, your occupation and your spouse.

We were bicoastal, but our shores were the Atlantic and the Gulf of Mexico. Every summer we'd pack up the family station wagon and trek 700 miles to the other end of the state, where our grandparents had a rustic compound on a bluff overlooking Pensacola Bay. I liked everything about this part of Florida. Pensacola had been around for 400 years. Its streets were lined with moss-draped oaks, Cracker cottages and Victorian homes with wraparound porches. We had relatives with double names, whose honeyed voices turned syllables into soliloquies. Everyone seemed to have plenty of time to sit around, nurse their drinks and voice their suspicions about life and each other. Miami had jet set aspirations; Pensacola seemed content to be itself. But the same kind of progress that had eaten up South and Central Florida was munching its way up the panhandle like a giant Pac-Man. In preparation the local tourism boosters had re-branded the region the Emerald Coast, hoping people would forget the old moniker, the Redneck Riviera. I decided it was time to head for the hills. I broke my folks the news that I was going to West Virginia University to get a masters degree in social work. I hoped the grant I'd landed to cover this education would soften the blow.

"West Virginia?" my father asked dubiously. He'd grown up in Springfield, Missouri, in an era when visiting dignitaries were presented with the Ozark Hillbilly Medallion. He'd spent a lifetime trying to distance himself from these roots, flying for the Navy in World War II, then marrying a Florida girl and working his way through law school at the University of Miami. By the time their three children had come along he'd transformed himself into a model of urbanity. He subscribed to the New Yorker, the Wall Street Journal and Playboy; he wore Italian loafers; he smoked cigars; he collected jazz; he'd spent a flight from New York to Miami chatting with Ernest Hemingway. And now, irony of ironies, his oldest son wanted to go back to the hillbilly roots. "There's nothing in West Virginia," he assured me. "I was there once. It's just mountains and trees."

"I *like* mountains and trees," I insisted. I explained that the program at WVU specialized in social work in rural areas, and since I was attracted to this kind of life, it seemed to make sense to go to school there.

"Social work?" he questioned the other half of my plan. The only social workers he'd ever met were on witness stands, testifying about unholy messes and wretched horrors. "You should be a psychologist instead. They make more money." I pointed out that social workers weren't deskbound, and they were interested in social justice. He wasn't impressed. "It's an oddball way to make a living."

"It's not like I want to be a shepherd in Romania."

"West Virginia, Romania - what's the difference?"

My mother saw things a little more philosophically. "I can see you doing that," she said.

"Herding sheep in Romania?"

She smiled. "Herding people in West Virginia."

It was the parental blessing I needed. I packed my Jeep and headed for terra incognita with Alfie, my Old English Sheepdog.

At WVU I made friends who spent their weekends backpacking, kayaking, skiing and playing bluegrass music. Two of my classmates had founded the state's first environmental group, the West Virginia Highlands Conservancy, and they enjoyed showing a Florida boy what mountains and whitewater looked like. Another classmate commuted to school from his farm. He showed up one day with a raccoon sandwich and gave me half of it. We went bird hunting on his farm and I bagged three quail. His mother turned our modest harvest into dinner, and I discovered that a quail has about as much meat on it as a field mouse. It seemed like an awful lot of work for an awful little food, but I guess that's why there weren't many fat pioneers.

I was drawn to the state's eastern highlands, where the Alleghenies straddled the two Virginias. A land of two, three and four thousand-foot ridges carpeted with woodlands, gentle valleys, rolling farms and sleepy little towns, this part of the state was becoming popular with people fleeing the East Coast's metropolitan sprawl. But they were flowing into the region in a trickle, not a gusher, and they weren't looking for high-rise condos. They were looking for the same thing I was.

I decided to stay in West Virginia after I finished school. I started driving around the eastern part of the state on weekends, checking out places where I could put down roots. Two towns ended up at the top of my list. Shepherdstown, a 250-year-old college town on the Potomac River, was close enough to Washington that it was part of the metropolis, but far enough away that it had its own thing going. Four hours to the south, in the middle of a broad agricultural valley, Lewisburg was a postcard of small town America, the home of the State Fair, and near the historic 6000-acre Greenbrier resort. I imagined myself living happily ever after in either place.

"I'm staying here after I graduate," I broke my folks the news in a phone call. People who aren't familiar with the Mountain State sometimes have mental images based on stark Depression Era photographs of grinding poverty, and it's hard to convince them this isn't an accurate contemporary portrait. Sure there were pockets of poverty, but there were plenty of folks living perfectly comfortable lives, and a tourist industry based on outdoor recreation was changing the state's image.

"We're moving to Pensacola," my father threw me a curveball. "Your grandparents are getting up in years and we need to be close to them."

"Great."

"Some of your cousins are moving back, too," he upped the ante. He ran through a roster of relatives flocking to the Gulf Coast like Israelites to the Promised Land. "It seems like everyone wants to live in Florida."

"Yeah, that's the problem," I said.

It would take another year and a fiancée to lure them to the scene of the crime, but when they visited West Virginia they were pleasantly surprised. "This is more civilized than I imagined," my mother said as she sipped Scotch on a cottage porch at The Greenbrier. I didn't tell her about the raccoon sandwiches. I was pretty sure the resort didn't serve the Other Dark Meat.

During grad school I served an internship in Pocahontas County. Rugged, remote and picturesque, Pocahontas is the northernmost county drained by the 173-mile long Greenbrier River. The university had arranged a job for me with the Department of Health and Human Resources in Marlinton, the county seat, but my real education came from my neighbors.

I was living on the river in a one-room hunting cabin I rented for $90 a month. I like to think of this as my Thoreau Period, but I had a few distractions Henry didn't have at Walden Pond. The local scarlet lady, Priscilla Lilly, lived on the hill behind me, in a shanty obscured by brush and tall weeds. Priscilla was single, with six children by four fathers. The county's social service agencies had beaten a well-worn path to her door for years, only to decide that Priscilla was more interested in a handout than a hand up. They'd pretty much given up on her.

Three young Lillys descended on my cabin the day I moved in. They played with my dog and watched with interest as I unloaded a small TV. They correctly predicted I wouldn't get any reception with the rabbit ears. Mommy can fix this, they promised. They disappeared and soon reappeared in the company of a short, squat woman in a John Deere cap. She was carrying a tangle of wire coat hangers. She whipped a pair of pliers from the back pocket of her jeans, dropped to her knees and went to work. I watched with interest as my new antenna rose like a phoenix from the ashes. I installed the contraption on the roof following the instructions she barked from below. I still didn't have any reception, but I'd gained an interesting sculpture and some unusual new friends.

Unlike at least four others, I found Priscilla's charms easy to resist, but she gave a social work student plenty of food for thought. Priscilla considered Welfare Mother her occupation and she wasn't interested in finding another one. She didn't suffer the nagging guilt Americans are supposed to feel when they aren't pulling themselves up by their own bootstraps. DHHR's many efforts to sell her on the beauty of the Work Ethic had fallen on deaf ears. At one point they'd supplied a chore worker to teach her how to keep her house. She viewed this cheery woman as a free maid, and she saved her dirty laundry, pots, pans and dishes for her visits. The optimistic worker became a bitter pessimist - Priscilla had that kind of effect on people - and she stopped coming. Priscilla had an encyclopedic knowledge of her government entitlements, and she was pleased whenever any of her children tested positive for the medical, psychological or educational conditions that allowed her to sample more freely from the smorgasbord of public assistance. She was a poster child for the excesses that would lead to the reform of the welfare system under the Clinton administration in the 1990's.

Priscilla spent a lot of time running around. She had more appointments than the CEO of a Fortune 500 company, and she didn't have a car. Since I drove into town every day she saw me as a handy resource, and she pressed me into service. She was as busy as a suburban soccer mom, but her kids didn't play sports or take ballet or act in church plays; they went to medical appointments and psychological assessments. I didn't know what to make of her. Our worker bee nation has never known what to make of its Priscilla Lillys.

I was talking with a coworker about my neighbor and he surprised me with the news that they had graduated from high school together. I'd assumed she was a dropout and I peppered him with questions. She'd been pretty ordinary back in high school, he assured me. The next day he showed up with a yearbook to prove it. It was a revelation to see that once upon a time Priscilla had belonged to the Future Homemakers of America and that she'd wanted to become a registered nurse. She wasn't the kind of medical caregiver I would have chosen, but it was interesting to know that she'd had aspirations. I decided the yearbook would make a good therapeutic tool, so I borrowed it and that evening I took it up to her shanty.

We sat on her lumpy, grease-stained sofa and paged through her glory days. She laughed and she oohed and she aahed. She offered comments about her teachers and classmates. She was tickled pink, having a grand old stroll down Memory Lane. She didn't seem to notice the vast gorge between what might have been and what had come to pass. I decided to help her out.

"So you were a Future Homemaker, huh?"

"Yep. Had Miz Hampton for Home Ec."

I imagined poor Miz Hampton turning in her grave. "Did you like that kind of stuff, Priscilla? All that sewing and cooking and canning?"

"Yep. Loved it." She flipped to a picture of herself at the senior prom. "Made my own prom dress," she said proudly. Then she added with a sigh, "That was the night I got pregnant with Delbert." On what turned out to be the first day of the rest of her life, her prom date had fathered her first child, who was now fourteen. The social service system had stepped in to lend a hand, and six children later, society's safety net had become society's spider's web.

During the four months I worked in Pocahontas County, Lilly kids turned up on my doorstep at all hours. Del was interested in the guitar and I taught him to play *Proud Mary*. Leo and Logan liked to fish from the rock outcropping below the cabin. They harvested hellgrammites from under the river rocks to use for bait, and they considered the bugs' nasty bites part of the sport. Freckle-faced Daisy, who liked to read and earned straight A's, was the family misfit. She talked a lot about Mrs. Lamb, her teacher the previous year, so I decided to pay this woman a visit and see if she could offer any insights into the Lilly clan.

Sally Lamb was the kind of teacher whose concern for her students extended beyond the classroom. She'd recognized Daisy as a flower in a garbage pail, and she'd hired her to babysit her three-year old. The Lambs had even taken Daisy to Walt Disney World during the Christmas break, staying with friends on the way down and back so she could see how other families lived. They'd devoted seven months to Project Daisy when something happened that had given them second thoughts. Daisy had entered a Mother's Day essay contest sponsored by a local supermarket. Her winning essay, *The World's Greatest Mother*, an ode to Priscilla's imaginary virtues, had scored the family $100 worth of free groceries. The Lambs took a much dimmer view of the World's Greatest Mother. They couldn't understand how Daisy could see her flawed parent in such a glowing light. Convinced their efforts were doomed to failure, they redirected their charitable impulses to adopting an orphan from the Third World.

"Consider the lilies," Jesus had exhorted his followers. I left Pocahontas County considering the Lillys, and from time to time I still do. I'm not sure what I learned from them, except that my education as a social worker was just starting. I do know one thing: if Henry Thoreau had lived next door to Priscilla Lilly, *Walden* would have been a far different book.

Chapter 3
Hard Knocks

While Priscilla Lilly was filling in the gaps in my education, some of my classmates were attending their own versions of the School of Hard Knocks.

Tina was from Pittsburgh. When the agency where she was serving her internship sent her on home visits she had trouble finding her clients. Her supervisor recognized that Tina had a poor sense of direction, so he started keeping her busy at the office. She returned to the university at the end of the semester feeling very frustrated. "Huntington's just so *confusing*," she complained.

"Huntington's the flattest city in West Virginia, Tina," I begged to differ with her. "And the easiest one to navigate. All the avenues run east and west, and all the streets run north and south. And they're numbered – 5th Avenue, 14th Street. What's so confusing about that?"

She gave me the kind of puzzled look Einstein probably got when he was holding forth on the Theory of Relativity. "But how can you tell which way is which?"

"If you watch where the sun comes up in the morning you'll know which end of town is east. You can orient yourself from there."

She gave this some thought. "You mean the sun rises in the east *every* day?"

I realized the scope of Tina's problem and I gave up. Social work isn't the best calling for the geographically clueless. Tina was going to need an office job or a chauffeur.

Another classmate, Cynthia, was telling me about her fieldwork in the state's southern coalfields. She'd grown up in a New Jersey suburb, and the coal miners' way of life was more than a little foreign to her. She was describing a family whose living conditions had shocked her.

"They lived in this tiny little place right next to a railroad track," she reported with wide eyes. "It sounded like the trains were coming through their house! And right in the middle of the living room they had this big metal ..." she searched for the right word, "... *thing*. There was something burning inside of it. It was so hot I could hardly breathe."

"A big metal thing?"

She bobbed her head. "It was up on legs and it had a big metal pipe coming out of it."

"It sounds like a woodstove or a coal stove, Cynthia. That's how they heat their house. I had a woodstove in the cabin I rented in Pocahontas County."

"Couldn't you just turn on the furnace?"

Somehow Cynthia had grown up without knowing there were homes without furnaces. Social work wasn't the best calling for the culturally clueless either. She'd had enough strange adventures. She quit the program, married a law student and lived happily ever after.

Mickey was our class brain. He breezed through subjects like Statistics while the rest of us were scratching our heads. But Mick was an introvert, and it should have dawned on him that an occupation with the word "social" in the title might not be a good fit. This didn't hit home until his internship at a Veterans Administration hospital in Clarksburg. He was a whiz at cutting through the bureaucratic red tape to help the vets, but he didn't enjoy having so much face time with them. He didn't like listening to their war stories. He came back to school and changed his focus to research, and he ended up teaching at a university in Ohio. He was a living embodiment of the old saw that "Those who can, do; those who can't, teach."

Sadly, my friend Jordan's social work career was permanently derailed. Jordan was an easygoing guy with shoulder-length hair, a recovering flower child. He was a quick study and an instinctive people person, exactly the kind of social worker you'd think any school would want to turn out. But he was selling pot to finance his education, and the chickens came home to roost when he was arrested two months before we graduated. It seemed like a gross miscarriage of justice to flog one student for the corporate sin, but that's the way the system sometimes works. He was honorable enough to refuse to name his clients, who included a couple of professors. But Jordan's entrepreneurial instincts served him well in the long run. He went into business and became a millionaire by the time he was forty.

Somehow I managed to avoid all the potholes and make it through the program. The ink on my diploma was still drying, but I was ready to cure the world of its social ills. I'm not sure why a quirky little mental health facility in the southeast corner of West Virginia seemed like the obvious place to start, but I headed to the Greenbrier Valley and reported for duty.

Chapter 4
Postcard from Tenerife

In its former life the building occupied by the Greenbrier Valley Mental Health Clinic had served as an overflow dormitory for the Greenbrier College for Women. When the two-year college closed its doors the state ended up with the property. Anne Blair, who was working out of a small office on Washington Street, finagled a deal with someone in the state bureaucracy to rent her the empty dorm for a dollar a year. This unusual history explained why the offices featured prominent sinks and medicine cabinets, and why bathrooms with tubs connected each suite. The clinic was a rabbit's warren of rooms, hallways and storage spaces. Disoriented clients could end up in sessions with the wrong therapists, or down in the basement, sharing their concerns with the janitor. The only redeeming architectural feature was the pine-paneled basement recreation room, outfitted with fireplace, kitchen, snack bar and booths. We held our weekly staff meetings in this cozy space. They usually took place on Tuesday mornings, but Anne Blair had moved this week's meeting to Monday so she could introduce me to my new colleagues.

"We have a postcard from Margo," she said as we made ourselves comfortable in a circle of mismatched chairs and rockers. She turned to me by way of explanation. "Margo Hodges is our clinical director. She's at a conference in the Canary Islands."

Africa's north coast seemed like a pretty far-flung place for a West Virginian to be attending a conference, but I had a lot to learn about

Margo. A compulsive traveler, our clinical director had discovered that some of the wealthier professional associations would foot the bills for their elected officers to attend their conferences. Inspired, she'd joined a host of obscure but well-heeled groups and set about politicking her way to high office. She used her various presidencies, vice-presidencies and secretariats to steer their meetings to the exotic climes she wanted to visit. She'd somehow managed to convince Anne Blair that all this globetrotting enhanced the clinic's reputation, and she rewarded her with a steady stream of Moroccan camel saddles, silk kimonos, Swiss chocolates, bottles of single malt Scotch and papal blessings. Margo was rarely present in the flesh, but she kept in touch by postcard. Her unused office looked like the den of a retired Secretary of State.

"Ola, Mi Amigos!" Anne Blair read this week's communiqué, which featured a colorful shot of a sprawling resort on Tenerife. "The Society for the Advancement of Psychodrama is keeping me so busy I haven't had time yet to explore this lovely island. Psychology and theatre aren't an inspired pairing. I'm spending my time dealing with the monumental egos of would-be actors and directors. On a more positive note, Richard Burton addressed our opening session. He invited me to attend the Cannes Film Festival en route to my symposium in Paris. Keep up the good work. You're always in my thoughts. Margo."

"Poor Margo," a sweet-looking older woman in a rocking chair chirped. "She's always on the go. That girl just doesn't know how to relax."

"Poor Margo!" a man with salt-and-pepper hair and wire-rimmed glasses scoffed. "That woman hasn't worked a day in her life! Why do we even pretend she's on the staff?"

Anne Blair shot him a dirty look. "Pete, for your information, Margo Hodges is one of the best-known psychologists in the world."

He wasn't impressed. "She should be. She's visited every country personally."

"You're just jealous, Doc," a young black man in a Navy blazer chided him. "You have a repressed desire to be Margo."

"You're damn straight. She's tossing back drinks on the Riviera while I'm medicating psychotics."

Anne Blair sensed it was time to move on. "We have a new social worker," she changed the subject. "This is Greg Johnson. Greg just finished his MSW at WVU."

We went around the circle and introduced ourselves. I didn't realize it, but I was meeting my new family. Anne Blair was single and childless, so she'd hired a surrogate family. Most of my colleagues were in their late twenties to late thirties; about the ages her own children would have been. Hazel Kessler, the woman in the rocker, was our grandmother-figure. Margo was our crazy aunt.

Hazel was the clinic's outreach worker. She visited clients at home, made sure they were staying on their meds, and provided transportation for those who needed it. Every Wednesday she whipped up an elaborate noonday meal in the clinic's basement kitchen and fed the masses, including most of our staff.

The grumbler was our psychiatrist, Peter Ableman. Pete hailed from Brooklyn and he didn't suffer fools gladly. Quietly listening to patients with Freudian detachment wasn't his thing. If they were acting like idiots he didn't mind telling them so. His opinions were reinforced by the Ivy League medical degree hanging on the wall behind his desk.

The young man in the blazer was our business manager, Cornelius Norman. Corny's superior intellect and razor-sharp wit had earned him a full ride at Georgetown University, where he'd picked up a business degree and impressive bartending skills, but where he had failed to acquire ambition. Anne Blair had encountered Corny at a party, his natural habitat, and she was intrigued that he'd managed to reach thirty without ever having held a job. She'd created the position of business manager for him so he could feel like he was making a contribution to society. There was little business to manage, which suited Corny perfectly. This left him time to read the newspaper and fill in his social calendar.

Our movement therapist, Penelope, was sitting in a half-lotus on the rug. Penelope had arrived in the valley with the Mother Earth News crowd, planning to be a self-sufficient homesteader. She'd quickly rediscovered the joys of electricity and toilet paper and taken a day job to be able to afford them. I asked her what a movement therapist did and she explained that she helped people get in touch with their bodies. This seemed a little vague, but so did Penelope.

It was pretty obvious the clinic didn't have a dress code. Anne Blair was wearing a Mexican peasant smock, which she'd accented with a strand of gumball-size fake pearls. Penelope had on some kind of body stocking. Hank Morgan, our substance abuse counselor, was wearing bib overalls. His fashion statement made more sense when Hank explained that he also raised beef cattle. Dealing with livestock required the same kind of patience that dealing with drunks and cokeheads did, so the two vocations actually worked together quite nicely for him. Hank liked to slip away from the office mid-afternoon to tackle his farm chores. Callers who thought they were being assured that he was outstanding in his field were actually being informed that he was out, standing in his field.

Our receptionist, Jayne Childers, was sitting next to me, scribbling on a steno pad. I thought she was taking the minutes of our meeting, but when I managed to steal a peek I saw she was working on her grocery list. Jayne was a sweet Southern charmer, and her natural ease with people made her an ideal front office person for a mental health facility.

We finished our introductions and Corny seized the floor. "I hate to bring up an unpleasant subject," he said apologetically, "but once again the dragon of destitution is breathing down our necks."

Anne Blair gave him a puzzled look. "What are you talking about, Corny?"

"The wolf of want is nipping at our heels," Corny stuck to metaphor.

"How about the iguana of insolvency?" Pete asked. "Is he sticking his tongue out at us?"

"The iguana is enjoying himself greatly at our expense. Our cupboard is in roughly the same shape as Old Mother Hubbard's."

This got Penelope's attention. She untangled herself from her yoga position. "Corny, I hope this doesn't mean we're not getting paychecks this week."

"We're all getting paychecks," he assured her. "But once you cash them we'll only have two grand left to make it from now to the end of our fiscal year on June 30th. I don't know how we're going to meet the payroll and keep the lights on."

Anne Blair looked shocked. "Two thousand dollars? That last report said we had $33,000!"

"That figure was in parentheses, Anne Blair," he explained. "Parentheses are the same as red ink. That's how much we've borrowed against our $35,000 line of credit. We're nearly tapped out."

"We've got to do something," she resolved.

Hazel entered the discussion. "Let's have a bake sale," she said brightly. "I'll make my pineapple upside-down cake."

"It's going to take a lot of upside-down cakes to make $35,000," Anne Blair said. She looked at me. "Maybe this isn't the best time to be adding a new staff member."

"I'll make brownies," I offered.

"I had a client who made a lot of money selling brownies," Hank remembered. "We can write to him at the federal pen and ask for his recipe."

It was gallows humor. A gloomy cloud hung over the room. "Didn't we have the same problem back in October?" Pete asked. "What did we do then?"

Corny made an unpleasant face. "Anne Blair sent me to Charleston to grovel. I had to listen to lectures about belt-tightening from 300-pound bureaucrats."

"They must have given you the money," Pete said. "We're still open."

"They gave us a supplemental appropriation along with the requisite tongue lashing. I don't want to have to face those people again. They hate us. We're the only freestanding mental health center left in the state. They want to regionalize us with the surrounding counties. They want to appoint an overseer and make us part of their plantation."

"What's stopping them?" Penelope asked him.

"Anne Blair," Corny revealed. "They think she's got some sort of in with the governor."

"We have our friends," Anne Blair hinted mysteriously.

"Remember their birthdays," Corny urged her. "Send them flowers and chocolates."

"I'll do my part," she promised. "Meanwhile you do yours. Go back to Charleston and grovel."

"Oh please God no, Anne Blair. Not again. I feel like Ned Beatty in *Deliverance*."

"Isn't that your job, Corny?" Penelope asked pointedly.

"Being sodomized by state officials? No, I don't believe that was in my job description."

Hank's eyebrows went up. "You have a job description?"

"No, but if we ever get around to writing them, boot licking isn't going to be one of my duties."

"I didn't enjoy it either, Corny," Anne Blair said. "That's why I hired you."

He whimpered.

I'd been following their conversation like a volleyball match. I could see that my new place of employment operated on faith-based budgeting. "So do I have a job or not?" I needed some final word.

Anne Blair reached over and gave me a pat on the knee. "Of course you have a job. But ask me again when Corny gets back from Charleston."

"Go, Corny," I cheered him on. "Only my whole future depends on you."

"Then you're in deep doo-doo," he warned me. "Anne Blair, are you authorizing me to wheel and deal with our overlords? Can I offer to trim next year's budget in exchange for cash in hand? Can we toss them a sacrificial lamb? What about Margo's position? We can live without her."

"We *do* live without her," Pete said.

"Margo Hodges will be the last person to leave this clinic," Anne Blair said with an air of finality.

"I realize she brings us immense prestige," Corny played along with the fiction. "But we need to look at all our options."

"Eliminating Margo is not an option."

"We're carrying a ghost on the payroll," he complained.

"Oh for Pete's sake, Corny, don't be so naïve."

"I'm not being naïve, Anne Blair. I'm being perfectly rational."

"Margo Hodges is the governor's cousin," she informed us. You could have heard a pin drop. And with that our fearless leader picked up the postcard from Tenerife and declared our meeting over.

We returned to our offices with a deeper respect for our founding mother and a renewed appreciation for dear Margo, our most valuable player.

Chapter 5
Gone with the Wind

Anne Blair assigned me to serve as the clinic's crisis worker in addition to seeing clients for therapy. This sounded pretty straightforward, but in practice it meant I was the go-to guy whenever one of my colleagues wanted to avoid some unpleasant or inconvenient task. I was getting my office set up when I had my first taste of this. The intercom buzzed. It was Hank, our substance abuse counselor.

"Welcome to the clinic," he said.

"Thanks, Hank."

"Are you busy?"

"Nah, I'm just unpacking books and shoving furniture around."

I thought he was going to suggest that we grab lunch, but he had something else in mind. "There's a gentleman in my office who wants to sign himself into the alcohol treatment unit at the Veterans Hospital," he said. "He needs a ride. I'd take him myself, but I've got another client waiting."

I didn't know Hank well enough yet to suspect that his other client was waiting on four hooves in the middle of his pasture. "Which VA are we talking about?"

"Salem, Virginia. Right next to Roanoke. It's not far."

I knew the geography well enough to know that "not far" meant a four-hour round trip. I realized Hank was Tom Sawyering me into whitewashing his fence, but the sky was blue, the dogwoods were in bloom and a drive over the mountains seemed preferable to spending the afternoon getting my office set up. "Sure, I'll do it."

"Good man. They're holding a bed for him. Just take him to Admissions and he can sign himself in."

"This guy's not a problem or anything, is he?"

"Major Bob? Nah, he's gentle as a lamb."

"Major Bob?"

"Retired. He played trumpet in the Army band for twenty years. You'll love him."

"Okay, I'll be down in a minute."

"No rush. Take your time."

I liked my second floor office, with its view of Church Street and the leafy campus of the former women's college. When the school closed, Anne Blair had conducted a clandestine raid and scavenged some odds and ends. Her prize was Apollo, a life-size nude statue Hank and Pete had lugged across the street and installed in the clinic's front entrance. A variety of seasonal decorations were employed to cover his genitals - a sprig of holly at Christmas, a spray of shamrocks on St. Patrick's Day, red, white and blue bunting for the Fourth of July. Apollo was the clinic's mascot, and a handy receptacle for hats, scarves and umbrellas.

I went downstairs to Hank's office. The door was open and I could see a middle-aged man with tousled hair sitting on the other side of the desk. He looked more like J. S. Bach than G. I. Joe. I hoped this meant we could talk about music, not Vietnam. Hank motioned for me to come in. "Major Bob, this is Greg," he introduced us. "You're in good hands."

Major Bob rose slowly from his chair and zigzagged in my direction like a tacking sailboat. Hank had conveniently forgotten to mention that the Major was two sheets to the wind. His right hand was adrift and I snagged it and gave him a handshake. "I'm the one taking you to the hospital," I explained.

His eyes grew wide. They looked like a Key West sunset. "The hospital?"

"The Salem VA, Major Bob," Hank refreshed his memory. "This whole thing was your idea. Remember?"

"It was?"

"One hundred percent." Hank came from behind his desk, placed his hands on his client's unsteady shoulders and looked him in the eyes. "You came in here 15 minutes ago and told me you'd fallen off the wagon and wanted to go back into treatment. Remember?"

As the Major considered this I had an unsettling thought. "Suppose we drive all the way over there and he changes his mind, or they decide he's not competent to sign himself in? Then what?"

"Piece of cake. You sweet-talk Major Bob or you sweet-talk the folks in Admissions or you bring him back here."

This all sounded pretty iffy, but I reminded myself that I could be playing a role in this man's recovery, even if it was only that of taxi driver. "Come on, Major Bob," I latched on to his arm and steered him to the door.

The Major marched on rubbery legs. With some effort we reached a small landing where three steps led down to the entryway. He eyed the steps like I was asking him to descend the Matterhorn. "Careful," I warned him. He stuck out an exploratory foot and missed the first step entirely, sending us both crashing to the floor below. The noise brought Jayne from her office. "Oh," she said, looking relieved. "I thought Apollo fell over."

"Thanks, Jayne. We could have broken bones and be bleeding internally, and you're worried about the statue."

"You know how Anne Blair loves that thing." She opened the front door for us and I escorted Major Bob outside.

It was a beautiful day. I'd taken the ragtop and doors off the Jeep and left them at home. "If nothing else, you'll get plenty of fresh air and sunshine," I promised the Major as I buckled him in the passenger seat. The quickest way to Salem was via the interstate, but I'd already decided to take the more scenic route, through Monroe County and over Peters, Potts and Catawba mountains. It seemed like a good opportunity to see the backcountry.

We were barely out of the city limits when Major Bob nodded off. He snoozed blissfully for 45 minutes until we began to climb Peters Mountain. He came to and studied our surroundings with a puzzled expression. I could see he didn't have a clue what he was doing in my Jeep, so we went back to Square One. "My name's Greg. I work at the mental health clinic. I'm taking you to the VA so you can sign yourself into treatment. Does any of this sound familiar?"

"Not really," he admitted groggily.

"We're on our way to Salem. We're in Virginia, between Paint Bank and New Castle." He seemed to be trying to take all this in. "Hank said you used to play trumpet in the Army band. Do you still play?"

"I play in a little combo," he said. "We're in the musicians union. We play parties mostly. We get union scale and free drinks. You can't beat that."

"Is that what happened to you last night?"

He thought about it. "No, I was home watching *Gone With the Wind*," he recalled. Without warning he burst into the movie's theme. "Da DA da da, da DA da da."

"You've got a nice voice," I complimented him.

"Da DA da da," he continued to serenade me, "Da DA da da, da DA da da. You know, *Tara's Theme* has got to be one of the most beautiful melodies ever written. Da DA da da ... "

Pretty soon he lullabyed himself back to sleep. The next time he woke up we were in New Castle. The little hamlet was home to fewer than 200 souls, but Craig County, Virginia, was so sparsely populated that New Castle was the county seat. He gave me a blank look and I could see we'd gone from Square One to Square Zero. I started to review the basics again, but he interrupted me and said he had to take a leak.

We pulled into a gas station and he disappeared in the rest room while I topped off the tank. Long minutes crawled by. Major Bob seemed to be taking a major leak. I grew suspicious. I went over to the men's room and knocked on the door. There was no reply. I banged on it. Still nothing. I called his name. There was no answer.

Worried that he'd given me the slip, I asked the attendant for another key. As luck had it he couldn't seem to find one. There was an open transom over the door, so I dragged an empty oil drum over, climbed up on it and looked inside. The Major was slumbering peacefully on the toilet.

"GROUND CONTROL TO MAJOR BOB!" I tried to get his attention. "WAKE UP, MAJOR BOB!" My voice echoed on the tile walls but failed to rouse him.

A beanpole of a teenager was walking by the station. "Hey!" I called to him. "You want to make a quick two bucks? My friend fell asleep in the restroom. I need you to crawl through this little window and open the door."

The boy came over and sized up the situation. With the effortless grace of an Olympic gymnast he hopped up and slithered over the transom. Seconds later he opened the door. The Major was still dead to the world, unaware of this aerial assault.

"What's wrong with this dude?" the boy wanted to know. "Is he like drunk or something?"

"Yeah, he's like what you don't want to be when you grow up," I gave him a little advice along with his two dollars.

The attendant suggested trying to get some black coffee into Major Bob. He fetched a Styrofoam cup with a foul-looking brew and we managed to pour some of it into his mouth. I don't know what they put in their coffee in New Castle, but he snapped to like we'd shocked him with defibrillator paddles. He was stepping spryly as we returned to the Jeep. We resumed his epic journey to sobriety and I took another stab at conversation. "What kind of music do you play, Major Bob?"

"Jazz mostly."

Jazz was my father's music, so I'd done my best to ignore it. I'd heard of guys like Dizzy Gillespie and Count Basie, but I couldn't have told you if they sang or played instruments, or the names of any of their songs. I was a jazz ignoramus. We needed another topic.

Major Bob came up with one. "You know what I think is the most beautiful song ever written?"

I had a hunch I knew where this was going. "No," I said, "but I'll tell you what *I* think is the most beautiful song ever written."

He studied me curiously. "What?"

"The theme from *Gone With the Wind.*"

His mouth fell open. I'd never seen a look of such pure astonishment on a person's face. "Are you shitting me? That's exactly what I was going to say!"

"Da DA da da," I sang, "da DA da da."

"Da DA da da," he chimed in, "da DA da da. Man, I can't believe you like *Tara's Theme*."

"I love *Tara's Theme*," I insisted. Actually I associated it with a sappy melodrama based on embarrassing Southern stereotypes, but I didn't want to rain on his parade. My mother was a big GWTW fan. She was a student at Florida State when this purple prose saga of the South had come out, and her Alpha Xi Delta sisters were so eager to read it that they ripped the pages from their sole copy and circulated it through the sorority house page-by-page. Because of her lifelong devotion to the book and movie, I knew more about Scarlett and Rhett and Ashley and Mammy than I knew about most of our relatives.

Based on our shared love of *Tara's Theme*, Major Bob decided we were kindred spirits. He grew more talkative. This was my first experience with the Road Trip Phenomenon, the tendency people have when they're on a journey to become increasingly open and candid. Road trips would play a significant role in my social work career. A vehicle is a rolling confessional, and when it comes to getting down to the naked truth, road trips work better than interrogation sessions, sworn testimony or psychiatrists' couches.

The Major became downright chatty. He was gay and he'd spent his life deeply closeted, afraid to come out because of his family's reaction and what it would have done to his military career. When he retired from the service he moved in with his mother. Since her death he'd been lonely and depressed and self-medicating with all the booze he could get his hands on. "I'd like to be a high school band director," he said, "but I figure most principals don't want to hire a queer drunk."

As he shared his tale of woe I had the feeling he was delivering this monologue more for his own benefit than for mine. I asked if I could pass this information along to Hank, but he was reluctant. He didn't want the counselors at the VA to know the score either; he thought his sexual orientation would count as a strike against him. "They'll stick it in my record," he was convinced.

Major Bob personified the problems facing gays in the 70's, especially in small towns. There were relatively few with Truman Capote's inclination to openly flaunt themselves. If you weren't independently wealthy, the price was too great. The helping professions were a step ahead of mainstream society in believing that sexual orientation was biological, but all we could do was be supportive and wait for the times to change. And have they ever. Now gays serve openly in Congress, mayors ride on floats in pride parades, and 14-year-olds come out to their teachers and friends and post their same-sex crushes on Facebook. Just about the only people left who seem to still need closets are Fundamentalist preachers and Republican officeholders.

By the time we reached the VA, the Major had sobered up. He signed himself in, we said our goodbyes and I encouraged him to drop by my office the next time he came to the clinic. We never saw Major Bob again. We heard he'd moved away, but no one knew where. I like to imagine him in San Francisco, strolling contentedly along Castro Street, whistling to himself.

I think I know the tune.

Chapter 6
Sam's Secret

My first clients were Roy and Emily Brown, who owned a dairy farm outside Lewisburg. After some friendly chitchat I asked about the nature of their problem. Emily reached down wordlessly, picked up a brown paper sack she'd set on the floor and handed it to me.

Roy was the strong silent type. His gaunt, chiseled face looked like it belonged on Mount Rushmore. He parceled his words with an economy that would have made him an ideal witness for the defense. ("Mr. Brown, didn't you find it an odd coincidence that your neighbor asked you to sharpen his ax on the same day his wife disappeared without a trace?" "Nope.") Emily was her husband's polar opposite, plump and chatty. She served as their spokesperson.

I shook the bag like it was a birthday present. "Should I open it?"

Roy nodded gravely. Roy would have gone down a waterslide gravely.

I unrolled the bag, looked inside and saw what looked like several pairs of women's panties.

"I found them in Sam's room when I was putting away his laundry," Emily said. "One's his sister's. We don't know where the other three came from."

"Sam?"

"He's our son."

"Did you ask him about it?"

"Lord, no! What was I going to say?"

With some probing I learned that Sam was a 16-year-old sophomore at Greenbrier East High School. Up until now his parents had considered him a perfectly normal teenager.

"It's just not right," Roy opined.

"Does his sister know about it?"

"Heavens no," Emily reacted. "What would we tell her?"

I explained that Sam needed to come to the clinic voluntarily, that our conversation would be private, and that I would share with them only what he gave me permission to share. This wasn't how they'd expected things to work, but they seemed to understand that Sam might speak more freely if he knew that what he said wasn't going to be repeated to his parents. "He'll be embarrassed when you bring it up," I tried to prepare them. "He'll probably throw a fit about you snooping in his room."

"I wasn't snooping! I was just putting away his laundry!"

"Yes, I understand that, but he'd probably rather talk about snooping than what you found."

"It's just not right," Roy said again.

I picked up Exhibit A and offered it to Emily.

She hesitated to accept the evidence. "Shouldn't you keep them for when you talk to him?"

"He's going to be uncomfortable enough without having panties dangled in front of him," I said. "And if he won't come in, I don't want to be left holding the bag."

Roy and Emily left with the unmentionables.

Three days later I was face-to-face with the lingerieto bandito. Sam was tall and lanky, with a toothy smile and sandy blond hair curling from under an Orioles cap. He looked like he'd put in plenty of time slinging bales of hay, but I couldn't help wondering what he had on under his Levis. "Thanks for coming in, Sam. You know why you're here, don't you?"

He shrugged. Young men have a dictionary of shrugs. This one meant *Hell yeah, but don't expect me to talk about it.*

"Anything you say here is confidential," I promised him. "If there's something I think your parents need to know, I'll ask you if I can talk with them about it. Okay?"

He gave me a skeptical look. "What if I say no?"

"Then it stays between us. It's your life."

"I'm not a perv, if that's what you think."

"There's no such thing as a perv, Sam," I said. "It's like calling someone a lunatic. There's no such thing as a lunatic either. They're just words people use to describe behavior they don't understand."

"Yeah, whatever. I'm not one."

"You look pretty normal to me."

"I *am* normal," he insisted.

"Then why don't you explain what those panties were doing in your dresser?"

He folded his arms. "Who says I've got to?" he challenged me.

"Nobody. But that's kind of why you're here, isn't it?"

"I'm here because my folks said they'd take away my truck if I didn't come," he clarified the situation.

"That's not how this is supposed to work. You should be here for yourself, not your folks. Why don't I give you a multiple choice to make things easier? Okay?" He didn't reply, so I offered him some choices. "A) You think girls' underwear is kind of a turn-on. B) Someone gave them to you. C) It was a prank. D) You like to wear girl's clothes. E) You feel like a girl trapped in a guy's body. Have I covered all the bases, or do you need more choices?"

I could see from the look on his face that I'd already given him more than enough. I thought he was going to opt for F) None of the Above, but he surprised me. "A."

"You think it's a turn-on?"

"Yeah."

"Are you worried about what your folks think?"

"Yeah. Wouldn't you be?"

"Are you attracted to girls or boys?"

"Are you callin' me a fag?"

"No. Do you want to talk about this or not?"

"I'm *not* a queer. I took 'em, and that's all there is to it."

"Because they're a turn-on?"

"Yeah. Big deal. So what?"

The scant information I'd managed to glean suggested I might be dealing with a sexual fetish. I didn't know anything about fetishes: they hadn't exactly offered courses on the subject at the university. I decided to stop talking about panties and start working on establishing rapport. "Why don't you tell me a little about yourself?"

At this point he would have been willing to discuss molecular physics if it meant changing the subject. I met a country boy who liked to hunt and fish, wasn't crazy about school and had a "sort of" girlfriend. He was active in his school's Future Farmers of America, but he couldn't picture himself milking cows for the rest of his life. He went into detail about his FFA projects, but we both knew we eventually had to return to the main subject.

I decided we'd gotten far enough today. "Sam, to be perfectly honest with you I've never dealt with something like this before. I don't even know if it's a problem. I'd like to talk with someone with more experience and see what I can find out. If you don't mind coming back next week, I'll tell you what I learn."

He gave me a wary look. "Doesn't Hank Morgan work here?"

"Yes. Hank's our substance abuse counselor."

"He knows my folks."

"I promise I won't talk to Hank, and if I talk to someone else I won't use your name. I'll call you Young Mr. X."

He gave me a thumbs-up. All things considered, our first session hadn't gone badly. He hadn't clammed up or walked out, which were distinct possibilities. I had a hunch he was curious about his own behavior, and that curiosity would bring him back.

As soon as he was gone I threw myself on the mercy of our psychiatrist, Pete Ableman. Pete was the most plainspoken member of our staff, blunt in the way only New Yorkers can be blunt. He enjoyed being cast in the role of oracle. "Sounds like a fetish," he agreed. "So what do you want to know?"

"Give me a mini-course in fetishes."

"Basically, we don't know shit," he summed it up. I liked Pete. He could have shown off his Ivy League education and given me a lecture about the etiology of fetishism, but he cut to the chase. He was the Harry Truman of psychiatry.

"Some underwear fetishists are turned on by the fabric," he took me to school. "They like the feel of the silk and nylon. Others are obsessed with one woman and they're only interested in the things that she's worn. That one's pretty obvious – the object's a substitute for the person. Others are into dirty laundry. They get off on the smell, the pheromones, like animals do. And some guys just get a rush from stealing naughty little trophies."

"Once I figure out what's motivating Sam, then what? Can you cure a fetish? Does it matter? Should I even bother trying?"

He took off his wire-rimmed glasses and polished them. "It's hard to cure something when you don't know what's causing it," he said. "At the risk of offending all the well-meaning therapists offering their services to fetishists, I don't think they're curable. But that's not to say they're not manageable. A fetish isn't necessarily a problem. Sex comes in lots of flavors. Your boy happens to like pistachio. If he thinks it's an issue, then it is. If he doesn't, maybe it's not."

"It's an issue for his parents."

"He won't live with them forever."

Pete's thinking was liberating, but Roy and Emily didn't seem likely to come around to having such refreshingly open minds on the subject. "Let's assume he wants to be cured. What are the alleged treatments?"

"Behavior mod and psychotherapy."

"That's it? No magic pills?"

He smiled. "People want to believe there's a pill for everything, and the pharmaceutical industry's only too happy to accommodate them. I'm sure that even as we speak, some researcher at Pfizer is putting little pairs of panties on laboratory rats."

It was an entertaining image, but I pressed on. "So if I want to use a behavioral approach, I need to zap him with a cattle prod every time he touches lingerie?"

"Basically."

"And if I want to go the talk therapy route?"

"You explore the reasons for his behavior and help him decide if he wants to change it. Of course that assumes he wants to spend weeks talking about it. Maybe it's like skin that freckles. Maybe it just is. Maybe he'll have to live with it."

"Any chance he'll grow out of it?"

"Absolutely. But there's a chance he won't."

I tried to imagine myself in young Sam's Nikes. He was following an urge that was essentially harmless, but one that could stigmatize him in the eyes of his family and friends. As fetishes went, underwear seemed preferable to sadism, exhibitionism and narcissism, but there was still a risk of public embarrassment. He needed to weigh the social costs.

"This is my first case, Pete," I reminded him. "I really want to help this boy."

"First you've got to decide what constitutes help in this situation."

Oracles like to leave you with riddles.

When Sam returned to the clinic I laid things out for him pretty much the way Pete had laid them out for me. He listened carefully, and then he made a confession.

"Sometimes I wear them," he admitted.

"How come?"

"They feel good."

"Okay. I appreciate your being honest about it."

"You said you wouldn't tell anybody."

"And I won't. I guess the bottom line is whether you want to try to do anything about this, Sam."

"Like what?"

"Do you think it's a problem?"

He took off his ball cap and his curly hair sprang everywhere. "If my friends find out they'll give me a pile of shit."

"So your main concern is people finding out?"

"Yeah. Seems like it's their problem, not mine."

"You don't want to try to kick the habit, so to speak?"

"You said I might grow out of it," he reminded me.

"True. But you might not."

He shrugged, suggesting he wasn't too worried about it.

"Sam, if that's the way you feel about it then you need to get sneakier. If you'd been more careful no one would have ever known."

"I can be sneakier," he assured me. "Problem is there's only two ways to get them - steal them or buy them. I'm not going shopping in some ladies department."

I hadn't considered the logistics. "Good point."

"Mom took my stash."

"So you're out of panties?"

He smiled. "Will you help me get more?"

I wanted to be a full-service social worker, but this seemed like a bit much. "No."

"You want me to be a thief?"

"You can go in a store and buy them, just like I can."

"Yeah, but you're old and you can say they're for your wife."

"A) I'm not that old, B) I don't have a wife, and C) when I do, she's buying her own."

"When I get married my wife and I are going shopping together."

"It's nice when couples have shared interests."

He gave me a concerned look. "So what will you tell my folks?"

"What would you like me to tell them?"

"Say I'm cured," he requested. "I mean, this is like my own business, isn't it? They'll never know."

"I'm not going to lie to your parents."

"Then just tell them something so they'll stop worrying."

"Like what?"

"You can figure it out."

I had a wrap-up session with Roy and Emily, and I honored the spirit of Sam's request. I told them their son had been very cooperative and honest and that we'd had three good sessions. I told them I'd consulted with our staff psychiatrist and that Sam looked like he was going to be fine. It was vague reassurance, but they seemed relieved.

Some therapists would take issue with my approach, which was to consider Sam the client and deal with things entirely from his point of view. They would argue that the family unit was the client, and that I should have educated Roy and Emily about the nature of their son's behavior. But this was my first case and I didn't know how to finesse it. Emily may have been educable, but Roy was rigid and he didn't seem likely to come around on the subject. Sam had a right to privacy, even from his well-meaning parents. As luck had it, things worked out. Thirty-plus years have passed and so have Roy and Emily. Sam and his sister sold the farm. He's an electrical contractor now, married with three children. Our paths cross from time to time and his sly grin suggests our shared secret. In retrospect I think he dealt with his situation in a healthy way. In the meanwhile a revolution has taken place in men's underwear. Now he can buy all the nylon and silk he wants without raising any eyebrows.

At our final session I gave him a parting gift that I'd gotten from J. C. Penney in Roanoke. I kept glancing over my shoulder at the checkout counter like I was making a drug deal. The hardest part was figuring out his size.

Chapter 7
New Kid in Town

Anne Blair was surprised when I decided to live in the town of Alderson. She was a lifelong Lewisburg resident and she couldn't understand why a young, single guy would choose Alderson, population 1100 (excluding the inmates at the federal prison where Martha Stewart would later take up residence), when the action was obviously fifteen miles up the road in Lewisburg, population 4600. The truth was simple: after two years of graduate school I was broke and the outlying communities had cheaper housing. Besides, I liked Alderson's setting on the Greenbrier River. Even with all its charms, the county seat didn't have a scenic river coursing through its heart.

I rented a trailer on a street lined with small, attractive homes. My green-and-white aluminum box was the neighborhood's ugly duckling, but the price was right and it came with a washer and dryer, which made it a little easier to overlook the warped paneling and swaybacked ceiling. I'd been there for a day when someone knocked on the door. I answered it and saw a large, impressive-looking black woman holding a cake. My dog Alfie came over to investigate.

She flashed a Cheshire Cat grin. "I heard we got a new neighbor," she said. "I made you a chocolate cake."

"Wow," I was taken by surprise. "Are you the Welcome Wagon?"

"Lord no, honey. The only wagons around here get pulled by horses in the Fourth of July parade. I'm Yvonne Standard. I live around the corner."

"It's nice to meet you, Yvonne. I'm Greg Johnson. I can't believe you went to so much trouble."

"Oh, sugar, it's no trouble. I've got six boys and I'm always in the kitchen. What's your doggie's name?"

"This is Alfie. He's friendly. Sometimes too friendly. Would you like to come in?"

"No thanks. I'm not one of those folks drops in out of the blue and hangs around all day. I've got a family and a job at the hotel, plus I'm starting my own church."

"I've never known anyone with their own church."

"The Mission of Deliverance Apostolic Jesus Name Church. We're only in a little storefront, but the Lord has bigger plans for us."

"It's nice to know I've got good neighbors."

"You've got a whole bunch of 'em." She pointed to a white two-story house across the street. "Martha Ellen and her two girls live over there. She's a nurse at the hospital."

I was curious about the older couple I'd seen coming and going from the brick ranch next door. "Who are my next door neighbors?"

She inched closer. "Donna and Leonard," she said in a low voice. "Now Donna, she's a sweetie, but that old Leonard's mean as a snake. I don't see how a nice woman like her ever got mixed up with a man like him."

"Maybe I'm mean as a snake, too, Yvonne. You don't know me."

She put her hands on her hips and gave me the once-over. "You look like a nice boy."

"I'm not exactly a boy," I said. "I'm getting up there in years."

"Honey, you don't even have wrinkles yet."

"I'm working on it. So when do I get to meet your family?"

"Don't worry, my kids'll be buggin' you soon. Hurry up and eat that cake before they see it."

"I will. Thanks again."

"*The Lord loveth a cheerful giver,*" she quoted Corinthians.

"Let's hope he loveth cheerful receivers, too."

"Oh, honey, you know he does."

And with that she strolled regally back up the street. I'm not sure how you define charisma, but Yvonne had it by the bucketful. I just hoped the cake wasn't a missionary effort to recruit me for her church.

Later that afternoon I was mowing the modest plot of grass around my trailer when I saw smoke coming from behind my neighbor's garage. I went over to investigate and found Leonard having a cigarette. He looked like a bulldog, with prominent jowls, a buzz cut and a stocky frame perched on bowed legs.

"What are you looking at?" he growled.

"I was just making sure your garage wasn't on fire."

He waved his cigarette. "Doc says these things are bad for my ticker, so I come out here where the wife can't see me."

I wasn't sure how this was helping his ticker, but I didn't pursue it. "My lips are closed," I promised him. "My name's Greg."

"I'm Leonard. Where do you work?"

"The mental health clinic in Lewisburg."

"*Mental health*," he snorted. "Any idiot with half a brain can solve his own damn problems."

"You'd think that, but someone's been keeping Dear Abby in business all these years," I countered. "I'm on call a lot. If you see me coming and going in the middle of the night, I'm not a serial killer."

"Thanks for the tip."

"What line of work are you in, Leonard?"

"I run the food service at the prison. I feed 900 of the meanest women in the US of A three squares a day. I used to run the mess at Camp LeJeune. I fed 1500 there."

"Were you a Marine or a civilian?"

"Civilian, my ass. Can't you tell a Leatherneck when you see one?"

"Yeah, you do kind of look like a turtle."

"That's leather*back*, you asshole."

"You cuss like a Marine."

He eyed my sandals. "Didn't your daddy ever tell you to wear shoes when you cut the grass?"

"I promise I'll be careful, Leonard. I'm pretty attached to my toes."

"You run around in those things, folks'll think you're a fairy."

"I grew up in Florida. Heterosexuals wear sandals down there."

"This ain't the beach."

Now that he mentioned it, since I'd left the university I hadn't seen many men wearing this kind of footwear. Apparently sandals had yet to arrive as a male fashion statement in working class Appalachia. Part of me wanted to say screw it, but another part wanted to fit in. "Thanks for the fashion tip, Leonard. I'll think about it."

Dealing with Leonard was a breeze compared to dealing with one of my other neighbors. Martha Ellen Burns and her daughters Ginny and Millie lived across the street. Sixteen-year-old Ginny looked like a Mediterranean beauty, and she was easygoing. Twenty-year-old Millie was a different story. She monitored my comings and goings from her second-floor bedroom window like a hawk watching a field mouse. I had a feeling she was sizing me up as boyfriend material.

I was washing my Jeep when she appeared in her front yard in a bikini, ostensibly to catch some rays, but it was five-thirty and the rays were fleeting. Her swimsuit left little to the imagination. Her thighs had more cottage cheese than the dairy section at the IGA, and her skin was the color of wet putty. She saw me staring and she waved.

I gave her a little half-hearted wave in return.

She bounded across the street like an eager St. Bernard and rested her ample arms on my chain link fence. "Pretty boring around here, huh?"

"I kind of like it," I said. "I'm thinking about joining the volunteer fire department."

"Alderson sucks," she shared her own take on things. "There's nothing to do here. God I miss Baltimore."

"Do you go to school there?"

"No, I was dancing at the Purple Pony."

"What's the Purple Pony?"

"A strip club."

It was hard to imagine an establishment with this low of an entertainment standard. It sounded like the kind of place where you'd be better off sitting on the curb, drinking Mad Dog from a paper bag.

"I had to quit when I got pregnant. I gave the baby up for adoption but they hired another girl in my place. So here I am."

So there she was. Millie was sharing the kind of intimacies most people save for their closest friends and I'd barely met her. This meant either she didn't have friends, or she didn't have discretion, or she wanted sympathy, or she was letting me know she put out, or all of the above. I tried to change the subject. "I figure the fire department's a good way to meet people, plus I can help the town."

"It was a boy," she continued her saga. "I never saw him. I knew if I did I'd want to keep him."

"They give you EMT training, too," I added quickly.

"Mom says I've got bad judgment. I don't have bad judgment. I'm just not ready to be a mother. I mean I'd definitely be a great one, but I don't want to have to take care of some baby. Is that so terrible?"

"Do you know when they have their meetings?"

She gave me a confused look. "What meetings?"

"The fire department."

Ginny told me that Millie had announced at dinner that night that the new guy across the street was weird. I hoped this meant I'd failed the boyfriend test, but I had a feeling it didn't.

I joined the Alderson Volunteer Fire Department and started taking first aid and CPR. The other firefighters were your basic salt-of-the-earth types who didn't mind doing the community's heavy lifting. Most of them had a congenital grasp of anything mechanical. When a new pumper truck arrived with an instrument panel that looked like the cockpit of a 777, they took a quick look and immediately intuited the functions of all the knobs, gauges and dials. Even young John, a member of the department's junior auxiliary, seemed to understand it all. (He grew up to become a cardiac electrophysiologist.) I looked at the same knobs, gauges and dials and realized the whole town could burn down before I could figure out how to start the sucker.

Our fire chief, Howard, had a deadpan sense of humor. He delivered all his pronouncements with a straight face, and punctuated them by spits of tobacco. After one house fire he described the only item we'd managed to rescue as "either her hope chest or some silver she's been taking from restaurants".

I liked hanging around the firehouse and dealing with challenges far different from the ones at the mental health clinic. With fires and car wrecks you knew what you'd saved and what you hadn't. At the clinic the rescues took a lot longer, and sometimes you never knew the outcome.

One Friday morning Ginny was waiting for the school bus and I was heading to work when Donna rushed out of her house. "Help!" she yelled frantically. "It's Leonard!" I followed her inside and saw Leonard flat on his back on the living room floor. He didn't look well. In fact he looked a lot like a corpse.

"Have you called the rescue squad?" I asked her.

"No! I just found him!"

"Call them. I'll do CPR."

I dropped to my knees and tried to remember what I'd learned in my classes. Donna hovered over us fretfully, waiting for her loved one to resurrect. Ginny stood in the doorway and watched with wide eyes as I alternated mouth-to-mouth and chest compressions until the paramedics raced in and took over. Howard's son H.R. was on the ambulance crew. He sized things up and gave me a barely perceptible shake of his head, letting me know Leonard was a goner. They loaded him in the ambulance and sped off with lights flashing and siren wailing.

Ginny was really shaken up. She'd missed her bus, so I offered to drop her at school on my way to work. We drove the twelve miles talking nonstop about what we'd just seen. The hospital was next to the high school, so I dropped her off and went over to the ER. The ambulance crew was just leaving. They told me Leonard had been pronounced Dead On Arrival, with cardiac arrest as the cause of death. He'd smoked too many clandestine cigarettes behind the garage.

That evening I confessed to Howard that I was afraid I might have performed the CPR incorrectly. He assured me that the procedure rarely restarts a stopped heart, and on the occasions it does, some patients suffer permanent brain damage. I thought he was just trying to make me feel better, but I've since learned that while CPR is useful, it's rarely the miraculous jump-start you see in the movies.

I attended Leonard's funeral at Johnson Memorial United Methodist Church. Martha Ellen and her girls showed up and Millie slid into the pew next to me and insisted on sharing a hymnal. This was a bad sign.

Donna decided to move in with her daughter in Asheville, North Carolina. She started downsizing, giving away or selling some of the things she couldn't take along. She gave me a beautiful oak clawfoot dining table, which was far and away the most valuable piece of furniture I owned for years. I still have it, and the oak has slowly mellowed to golden brown. Occasionally I imagine Leonard's ghost barking at me to get my faggy sandals off his clawfoot.

Chapter 8
With Dolly as My Co-Therapist

Corny's groveling at the state capital succeeded, and he returned with a supplemental appropriation to bridge our budget gap. This meant we didn't need to hold bake sales to keep our doors open, and for the moment my job was secure.

About the same time Anne Blair took a call from a 17-year-old girl, who complained that her father hadn't left their home in nearly a year. She dispatched me to Williamsburg, a farm community 20 miles away, to check things out. I expected to find a morbidly obese soul confined to his bed in a darkened room, but Tucker Blake was fit and tan and working in his garden. His house at the foot of Cold Knob could have been a country inn, with its wraparound porch, cupola and copper weathervane. He looked surprised when I appeared between his rows of cabbage. I explained that his daughter had called the clinic because she was concerned about him.

"Big deal," he shrugged it off. "So I'm a homebody."

"Annie claims you haven't been to town in a year," I repeated the tale. "She says she has to handle everything – the shopping, the banking, even the car repairs."

"I pay for it," he said with irritation. "Is there something wrong with teaching a girl to be independent?"

"No."

"Besides, what business is it of yours?"

"She's worried about you. Most kids her age wouldn't call a mental health clinic about anything."

He put his hoe over his shoulder and walked toward me. "You think I'm nuts? Are you sending the men in white coats to haul me off?"

"When we get a call like this we're supposed to make sure everything's okay."

"Everything's hunky dory," he assured me. "You don't have to worry about me."

"Okay. Sorry to bother you. Give us a call if we can ever help with anything."

As I turned around to leave he said, "Hell, maybe I am a nutcase."

I sat in a rocker on the porch and listened to Tucker's story. His wife had died of breast cancer a little more than a year ago. She was a beloved elementary school teacher, and after her death he was inundated by people offering their condolences and asking if he was okay. He was uncomfortable with all this attention, so he retreated to his home. He'd quit his job as a forester and was making ends meet with savings and his wife's pension and Social Security. He watched sports and busied himself with home improvement projects, which explained why the house looked like it belonged on the cover of Southern Living. Annie had reacted to her mother's death by immersing herself in the local theatre. She was always driving back and forth to town, so she'd become the family gofer.

"Where did you go the last time you went out?" I was curious.

"I went into the farmer's market to sell some produce. I got lightheaded and I felt like I was going to pass out and I was sweating like a pig. I could hardly breathe. I turned around and came back home. I guess you're going to tell me it was a panic attack."

"When was that?"

"Last August or September."

"Was that the only time it's happened?"

"Nope. It was happening every time I went into town. I figure it's easier to stay home."

I thought of a couple of possibilities. One was that he was having a grief reaction. Another was that he was suffering from post-traumatic stress. In either case it was manifesting the same way. "Have you ever heard of agoraphobia?" I asked him.

He smiled. "You too, huh? That's what everybody says I've got. But what's wrong with staying at home?"

"Nothing, as long as you can afford it and it's not messing up your life."

"I miss my job, but not all that much, if you know what I mean."

"What about Annie? It bothers her that you're living like this."

"She calls me a hermit," he said. "She wants to be an actress and she wants me to go to her plays. But if I can't even go to a farmer's market, I sure as hell can't sit in a damn theatre."

"There's a treatment that works sometimes with agoraphobia," I let him know. "It has an even bigger name than the problem: systematic desensitization."

"It sounds like a science experiment," he reacted.

"Not really. All it means is going back to town in baby steps."

One of our psychology professors at West Virginia University thought it would be interesting to give us the Minnesota Multiphasic Personality Inventory, a test developed in the late 1930's at the University of Minnesota, commonly known as the MMPI. The test consists of several hundred true or false questions that people with similar personality characteristics tend to answer in similar ways. You don't get the answers right or wrong; your answers theoretically display patterns that reveal your personality makeup.

Despite the MMPI's vaunted reputation and my curiosity about it, I hated taking this test. For every question I could answer right away ("I am very seldom troubled by constipation") there was one that gave me pause. I came to a screeching halt at, "I could be happy living all alone in a cabin in the woods or mountains." The idea had some appeal - a retreat for a couple of weeks, or even a month. So should I answer true or false? I thought about it from the interpreter's point of view. If I said true I'd sound antisocial. If I said false I'd look insecure. It seemed like a lose-lose proposition, so I answered both true and false. I proceeded to do the same thing with all the other questions that made me feel ambivalent. The professor wasn't pleased; he declared my results invalid.

Tucker Blake could have answered the "happy living all alone" question without even thinking about it, but instead of a cabin on a mountain, he had a beautifully restored farmhouse at the base of one.

The Greenbrier Valley Theatre occupied a rickety wooden structure called the Barn, next door to the Greenbrier Valley Airport. The Barn was a basilica of jackleg carpentry, cobbled together by Vista volunteers from outbuildings scavenged from surrounding farms. A garden hose trickled water over the tin roof, providing the kind of cooling system you'd expect to see in a Banana Republic. The actors shared their dressing rooms with groundhogs and skunks. When planes took off or landed next door, the performers would freeze until the roar of their engines subsided.

I found Annie in the props room, sewing a ruffle on an apron for *Fiddler on the Roof.* She looked like an actress, with high cheekbones, green eyes and butterscotch hair. I asked her why a performer was doing a techie's work.

"I'm both," she said as she continued sewing. "I'm the costume assistant and I'm Tzeitel, Tevye's oldest daughter."

"Paying your dues before you go to Broadway?"

"I hope. I'm majoring in theatre when I go to WVU."

"What's your dad going to do when you leave home?"

She paused in mid-stitch. "That's the problem. It's so stupid. It's like I'm the parent and he's the child. I'll probably have to drop out to take care of him." She explained that her father had never been very outgoing and that her mother's death had given him an excuse to withdraw.

"Annie, I can't change your dad's personality, but I might be able to get him out of the house."

She gave me a doubtful look. "How? Set it on fire?"

"When does your show open?"

"Three weeks."

"I'll have him here on opening night," I promised her.

Like many introverts, Tucker was perfectly comfortable one-on-one. When I dropped by he seemed to enjoy our conversations. He had a large fund of general knowledge from reading, watching TV and listening to public radio, and he held informed opinions on a wide range of subjects. Strangely, the subject that really got him going was Dolly Parton. He'd seen Dolly on *The Porter Wagoner Show* and he'd become an instant fan. In fact, he was a bit obsessed with her. When he tried to describe Dolly's physical attributes he fell into silent, head-shaking awe. Dolly was a little over-the-top for my tastes, but I kept it to myself.

To make any progress we needed to push the envelope, so ten minutes into our second meeting I told him that if he wanted to keep talking we needed to sit in the Jeep. He knew what I was up to, of course. With reluctance he followed me outside and sat in the passenger seat. The next time we met we drove a half-mile down the road. By our ninth meeting we were pulling into the gravel parking lot at the GVT Barn. He was jittery, but he put up with it because he liked having a sympathetic ear. He treated me like a buddy who dropped by to shoot the shit, and he always gave me a Dolly update. I wondered what his late wife would have made of this crush, but I didn't say anything.

The evening *Fiddler* opened I swung by to pick him up. He was in the garden in a T-shirt and shorts. "I'm not going," he said flatly. "I can't deal with all those people."

I'd pried him from the house, but I'd neglected to prep him for the social encounter. He knew his daughter would be disappointed, but he preferred the guilt trip to the road trip. I ended up going to the play by myself. After the show I found Annie to congratulate her and give her the bad news.

"I knew he wouldn't come," she said. "I know him a lot better than you do."

"How long does your play run?"

"Three weeks."

"I'm still going to get him here," I vowed.

"Good luck," she wished me. I could tell she didn't believe it.

Most mental health centers worry about billable hours and whether Medicaid or private insurance will cover the services they're providing. Anne Blair had a more humanitarian mindset, which went a long way in explaining the clinic's precarious finances. If a staff member wanted to devote hours and hours to a particular case with no hope for reimbursement, the fiscal implications weren't on her radar. It didn't bother her that I was devoting so much time and gas to Tucker.

Sometimes at the end of the workweek we would retreat to her home on Washington Street for a happy hour. My agoraphobic was the hot topic this week, and everyone seemed to have some advice to offer. The suggestions ranged from "He needs a nice church family." (Hazel) to "Just leave the poor bastard alone." (Pete). Anne Blair was more interested in my review of *Fiddler on the Roof* because she was going to see it on Saturday.

The following Monday I took Tucker to lunch. We ate at Jim's Drive-In, where we could eat burgers while we sat in the Jeep. This wasn't very threatening and he did fine. On Tuesday we went to the Pioneer Drug Store and sat at the soda fountain. The place was nearly empty, but we still counted it as progress. On Wednesday we ratcheted things up at Gwen's Kitchen, where Gwen generously ladled her home cooking onto plates from a stove in the back room. Students from the School of Osteopathetic Medicine came and went and Tucker got antsy. He scarfed his food down so we could hurry up and leave.

We suffered a major setback on Thursday when we ate lunch at the Court Restaurant. The scene was elbow-to-elbow, and Tucker was a nervous wreck. He was convinced he was having a heart attack and needed to go to the ER. "It's a panic attack, Tucker," I tried to reason with him. "Just because your heart's thumping and your breathing is constricted doesn't mean you're having a heart attack. Take a deep breath." He got up and headed for the door. I followed him outside. "Get a grip on yourself, man. You've got to beat this thing." But his panic symptoms had taken over and my reassurances were useless. I decided to switch gears. "Maybe you do need medical attention. We have a doctor at the clinic."

We went to the office and Pete shot him up with an anti-anxiety agent. Twenty minutes later his symptoms had subsided. He left the clinic with enough free samples to get through his daughter's play. But what had we gained? He'd pop the pills, see *Fiddler* and then go back being a recluse. The next day I expressed my misgivings about this to Pete.

"You can't give this guy a personality transplant," he brought me back to earth. "When his girl goes off to college, he'll have to go out or he'll starve. Nobody's going to go shopping for him. In the meanwhile I can put him on a low dose of something. That'll give him a reason to keep coming back here and you can work with him. But don't expect him to turn into a social butterfly."

"I'll be happy if he turns into a moth who only goes out occasionally at night," I said.

Pete's intervention was transformational. On Friday we had dinner at the Court Restaurant and went to the play. Tucker was so laid back, or drugged up, he even nodded off a couple of times during Act II. After the show he presented a beaming Annie with a dozen roses. It was a triumph for all involved.

A strange thing happened as we headed out to the parking lot. A woman who looked like Dolly Parton appeared out of nowhere, sashayed by us and disappeared inside the Barn. She had the same top-heavy figure and same overworked pile of blonde hair. Tucker was mesmerized. His eyes followed her into the Barn. "Who's that?" he asked me. "One of the actresses?"

"I have no idea," I said.

When I saw Annie the next day I mentioned this mystery lady and asked if she knew her. "Dad's been bugging me about her, too," she said. If you promise not to say anything, I'll let you in on a little secret."

I raised my right hand. "I swear on the collected works of William Shakespeare."

"It was one of my actor friends in drag," she revealed, looking very pleased with herself. "I put him up to it."

"Annie, you're a little schemer. Your dad's talking about coming back here to try to find her."

"That's the whole idea," she said.

We all had our methods, and I had a feeling hers were going to work better than mine.

Chapter 9
Driver Education

When local law enforcement got wind that the mental health clinic had a crisis worker, they decided they could call us whenever they had domestic matters that seemed unworthy of their time. A teenager punching a softball-size hole in his family's living room wall fell in this category, so I was summoned to the scene in the town of Rupert. When I arrived the responding officer beat a hasty retreat, like a tag team wrestler slipping out of the ring, leaving me with Tommy and Mary Jo Jensen and their son Rick, a sullen 16-year-old with his right hand wrapped in a gauze bandage.

Rupert is a small community on Greenbrier County's western end. The coal industry operates discretely in the nearby hills, out of sight and mind of the rest of the county, where agriculture and tourism are the mainstays. Tommy, a retired miner with black lung disease, was sitting in a recliner, breathing from an oxygen concentrator. Things were arranged within arms-reach around him and I gathered he didn't stray very far from his La-Z-Boy. Mary Jo offered me a chair and she took a seat at the other end of the couch where Rick was sulking. Short, tan and muscular, Rick didn't resemble either of his parents, although it was hard to say what Tommy might have looked like before he was wasted by his illness.

This was a night call, so I got right down to business. "Okay, Rick, what's the story? Why did you punch a hole in the wall?"

He shot his mother a dirty look. "She won't let me get my driver's license."

She reacted immediately. "Rick, I've told you a hundred times we can't afford the insurance. You know your father's sick and we have bills. Why is that so hard for you to understand?"

"I said I'd get a job!"

"Your father's not in any shape to teach you to drive. And you know what a nervous wreck I'd be."

He threw up his arms. "So what am I supposed to do? Bum rides the rest of my life? I'm the only guy in my class who doesn't drive."

"Does your school have driver's ed?" I asked him.

"She won't let me take it!" he continued his litany of abuse. "Even if she would, it's too late. The class is full."

"Rick needs to learn to drive," I took up his cause. "Is there someone else who can teach him? A relative maybe?"

"Uncle Larry," Rick proposed.

His mother scowled. "Your Uncle Larry's been arrested twice for DUI. He doesn't even have a license."

"He drives."

"You're *not* getting in a car with Uncle Larry."

Tommy looked like he couldn't muster the energy to join the discussion. Rick had a parent-and-a-half. I felt for this little family. Without thinking I made an impulsive offer. "I could teach Rick to drive. But my Jeep's a 5-speed, so he'd have to learn on a stick shift."

The young man glanced at his mother hopefully. "I need to learn to drive a stick anyway. I'm going in the Army when I graduate."

"Teach the boy to drive," Tommy rasped. He sounded like Don Corleone in *The Godfather*.

Rick was instantly repentant. "Sorry about the hole. I'll fix it tomorrow."

His mother looked very iffy about all this. "Well I still don't think it's a good idea. You need your birth certificate for your learner's permit and we don't have it."

"Where is it?" Rick asked.

"I don't know. I lost it a long time ago."

"I can order a duplicate," I offered.

"But he was born in California," she said in a way that suggested that this might be like trying to get one from Kuala Lumpur.

"No problem," I assured her. "I'll call their vital records office and order a certified copy. I just need his date of birth and your maiden name."

"We really can't afford to put him on our insurance," she continued to object.

"Mom! I said I'd get a job!"

"Why don't we just take it one step at a time?" I said. "He can get his license, and you can let him start driving when you can afford it." He'd badger them to death until they did, of course, but they could cross that bridge later.

Mary Jo and Tommy exchanged looks I couldn't quite read. Was there something they couldn't discuss in front of their son? Did he have an explosive temper or a drug habit or something else that meant he shouldn't be behind the wheel? Whatever it was, they kept it to themselves.

"When can I start?" he asked eagerly.

"That's up to your parents."

Tommy took a coughing fit and his face turned purple. I thought we might have to call an ambulance, but Mary Jo took it in stride. Eventually he caught his breath and raised a mottled hand. "Go ahead," he gave the driving lessons his blessing. "Get the birth certificate."

On the way home that night I thought about my own driver education. It was summer and we were staying in a rustic two-room cottage that our grandparents owned in Gulf Breeze, on a bluff overlooking Pensacola Bay. I'd just turned sixteen and I was bugging my father to teach me to drive. My cousins were driving, and that magic little plastic card from the state seemed to be what separated the men from the boys.

My father was a good driver but he wasn't a teacher by nature and he didn't have a burning desire to impart his skills to others. Complicating matters he was impatient. He didn't like instant gratification because it took too long. He approached teaching me to drive the way some parents approach teaching their kids to swim by throwing them in a lake and waiting for their survival instincts to kick in. He figured if he stuck me behind the wheel some Inner Driver would whisper the necessary instructions in my ear. This allowed him to read the newspaper while I wove in and out of lanes and tailgated the other cars so closely they could see the pupils of my eyes. I needed some pointers, but he didn't want to deny me the joy of self-discovery or himself the opportunity to catch up on the news.

I slammed on the brakes and we screeched to a stop. He glanced up from his paper and saw the rear end of a concrete mixer. He directed me up Highway 98 to a new subdivision that was under development. It had roads but no houses, which made it a perfect place to practice. Abandoned pieces of heavy equipment dotted the landscape but the streets were deserted. I dodged bulldozers and backhoes and pavers while he studied the sports section. When he finished the paper he announced it was time to go home.

"How'd I do?" I asked hopefully.

"Great."

"When's my next lesson?"

"There isn't one," he said. "You can take the test next week."

"You really think I'm ready?"

He didn't reply. I got the message: I'd exhausted his tiny reserve of patience, so I was deemed test-worthy.

On Monday we crossed the three-mile bay bridge that connected Gulf Breeze to Pensacola. The yellow cinderblock State Police station where the road tests were given sat near the foot of the bridge. We filled out the necessary forms and my father claimed a seat in the waiting room. I left with the examiner, a grim-looking trooper who presumably had the balls of steel necessary for his calling. We pulled out of the station and he told me to take a left. I complied. He grabbed the dashboard and braced himself, and I knew I'd already screwed up.

"It works better if you keep all four wheels on the ground when you turn the corner," he pointed out. "I think we'd better go back to the station."

"Already? We just left."

"Go back to the station."

"Does this mean I failed?"

"You're driving on the shoulder. Get back on the road."

"I don't want to hit the other cars."

"Good idea, but stay on the road, son. That's why they put it there." We'd barely left the station when we were back. "Park over there," he indicated a space between two cars.

I complied, and we ended up so close to the vehicle on the right that he had to climb out on the driver's side. He checked the Fail box with what seemed like unnecessary relish, ripped it from his clipboard and presented it to me.

"What do I need to improve on?" I asked gamely.

"Driving. You need a lot more practice."

"When can I take the test again?"

His pained expression suggested I was missing the point, but he gave me the legally correct answer. "Next week. If you come back, come on Wednesday."

"Will I have you again?"

"No. I don't work Wednesdays."

I went to the waiting room and showed my father the form. "He says I need more practice."

He winced and everyone in the room laughed. We went outside and he saw my parking job. "How in the hell did you do that?"

"The trooper told me to park there."

"Give me the keys."

"Can I drive home?"

"Get in the car."

I slouched into the family station wagon and slid over to the passenger side, where it looked like I was going to be spending the rest of my life. A couple of troopers cracked the Venetian blinds in the station and watched with interest as my father inched the vehicle out of the space with the intense concentration of a man defusing a bomb.

It seemed best to lay low for a while, so I reported to my cousins that I'd failed on a minor technicality. I let the rest of the week go by without asking to drive. In the meanwhile I started paying attention to what my parents did when they were behind the wheel. I noticed how they claimed intersections when they were making left turns and how they merged into traffic without stopping. I realized that both of my folks were good drivers. Hopefully it was hereditary.

The following week we returned to the scene of the crime. I'd only had one more practice session, but my Inner Driver was starting to whisper. Things went better this time, and the new examiner gave me a couple of pointers before telling me I'd passed.

I bounded into the waiting room brandishing the evidence of my achievement. My father took the document and studied curiously. As we drove back across the bay bridge he offered a bit of sage advice. "Let this be a lesson to you, Greg," he said. "You don't know how to drive, but you have a license. There are a lot of other idiots just like you on the road, so be careful."

An official-looking envelope arrived at the clinic from the California Department of Public Health, Office of Vital Records. When I opened it I was dismayed to see that some anonymous laborer in the bureaucratic vineyard had sent the wrong birth certificate. I was standing in the front office scowling at the form and Jayne saw I was upset.

"What's the matter?"

"I'm trying to help a kid get his learner's permit. I sent fifteen bucks off to the State of California, but instead of sending me Richard Jensen's birth certificate they sent me Richard Hernandez's."

"Let me see it." She studied the document with her practiced eye. "When was he born?"

"August 5, 1960."

"Who's his mother?"

"Mary Jo Martin."

"Who's his father?"

"Tommy Jensen."

"Unless Mary Jo Martin had two sons named Richard on August 5, 1960, this is his birth certificate."

"What?"

I followed her finger over to his father's name, Umberto Hernandez, and his occupation, engineer. "Tommy Jenson's not his father," she connected the dots for me.

"Holy crap." I remembered Mary Jo's reluctance about all this, and the weighty looks she and her husband had exchanged before giving me the go-ahead. In my eagerness to help, I'd opened a much bigger can of worms. "Now what am I going to do?"

She picked up a little white bottle and shook it. "I have White-Out and a typewriter. We can give him a new father in five minutes."

"That's probably some kind of felony, Jayne."

"I'm joking."

I called Mary Jo and told her we'd hit a snag with the birth certificate. She didn't seem surprised. I asked if we could get together when Rick wasn't home, and she told me to come on over. I found Tommy still ensconced in his recliner and things looking pretty much the same, except the hole in the wall had been patched and painted. "I see Rick's been busy."

His mother sighed. "He wants to drive so badly."

"I guess you know what I ran into."

She gave me a guilty look. "I've got the original certificate. You probably think I'm a terrible mother."

"No, I don't think that."

"You're a damned good mother," Tommy rasped.

"I was living in San Diego," she told me the story. "I met Umberto in the park one day. He was from Uruguay, in California working a bridge project. We saw each other a couple of times. When I found out I was pregnant he was already back in South America and I didn't know how to get in touch with him. I had Rick, and then I met Tommy and we got married and moved back to West Virginia."

"I came back from the Navy with a wife and a son, and I let on like he was my own," Tommy explained. "Everyone thinks I'm his father. We've always called him Jensen."

"And you've gotten by all these years without a birth certificate?"

"They asked for one when I enrolled him in kindergarten," Mary Jo said. "I told them I'd lost it and I promised I'd get another one. I guess they forgot about it. Every time I've needed one - Little League or whatever - I've been able to get around it. But it looks like there's no getting around it now."

"Does Rick know any of this?"

She shook her head.

"Where do we stand on the learner's permit?"

"The boy's got to learn to drive," Tommy said. "We've got to tell him the truth."

The school bus arrived and Rick came in. After he grabbed a snack his parents sat him down and gave him a more detailed version of the story they'd given me. He listened with a shell-shocked expression.

"Why are you telling me this now?" he asked them.

"There's a problem with your birth certificate," I said. I unfolded the document from California and handed it to him.

He studied it with a puzzled expression. "Who's Richard Hernandez?"

"You are, Rick. That's your legal name. If you're going to get your learner's you need to decide if you want to be Richard Jensen or Richard Hernandez."

With a young would-be driver's priorities, he asked, "Which is quicker?"

"Hernandez. You're already Richard Hernandez. If you want to be Jensen you'll have to go to court."

"How long's that take?"

"A couple of months, probably."

He shrugged. "If I'm Richard Hernandez, I'm Richard Hernandez." He turned to Tommy. "You okay with that, Dad?"

"Doesn't bother me a damn bit," Tommy said. "Call yourself whatever you want. You're still my boy."

Rick never looked back. He put on his new identity like he was changing shirts. He went to school the next day and told his friends to call him Hernandez. He informed his teachers that his mother was having his name changed on the school records.

I was determined to put more effort into Rick's driving lessons than my father had put into mine. For one thing, I had a better student. After popping the clutch twice he caught on to shifting. In no time he was gliding through the gears like he was rowing across a glassy lake. He listened to pointers and he accepted correction. He was a natural. After all, he was an engineer's son.

While Rick honed his driving skills, his father's pulmonary disease worsened. He entered the VA hospital in Beckley and he died in December, leaving his family to live on his miner's pension and Social Security. Mary Jo bought Rick a '66 Nova and he got a restaurant job in Lewisburg. Occasionally I'd see him burning up the road between Rupert and Lewisburg. He always slowed down and waved, and then he sped on his way.

Some people have a natural resilience that others lack, a capacity to roll with life's punches. Rick was a shining example. Years later, after he'd finished a hitch in the Army, I ran into him and complimented him on the way he'd handled what could have been a serious identity crisis. He shrugged it off.

"Could have been worse," he said philosophically. "I could have been Umberto, Junior."

Chapter 10
A Cold Bud and a Glass of Chardonnay

When it came to marriage counseling I tiptoed quickly and quietly in the other direction. I'd been working at the clinic for nearly three months, but I didn't feel like I could tackle marriage counseling with much authority. Since I'd never been married I didn't have much faith in my ability to navigate the tricky matrimonial waters. I heard someone give a speech once with the following litany:

If you want to be happy for an hour, take a nap.
If you want to be happy for a day, go fishing.
If you want to be happy for a week, take a vacation.
If you want to be happy for a month, get married.
If you want to be happy for a year, inherit a fortune.
If you want to be happy for the rest of your life, help other people.

When he delivered the line about marriage the people in the room who laughed the loudest were the ones who were married the longest. Gene, a fifty-one year veteran, nearly fell out of his chair. We practically had to give him oxygen. The younger people didn't get the joke.

I'd been successfully dodging marriage counseling at the clinic when I saw Jake and Grace Garland penciled in my schedule with the note "marital problems". I complained to Jayne, who pointed out that I had more openings than my coworkers, her gentle way of telling me to shut up and carry my own weight. "What the heck," I accepted my fate. "It won't be the first time I've totally screwed up someone's life."

Jake was bearded and burly, and wearing a Steelers jersey. He took the stairs two at a time, raring to go. Pixie-like Grace followed with decidedly less enthusiasm. "We've never done anything like this before," she said. "It feels awkward."

It did for me, too, but I didn't admit it. "A lot of people feel nervous the first time they come in," I tried to put her at ease. "Talking with strangers about your personal problems only comes naturally in bars and beauty shops."

"I've been doing that for years," she confessed.

Jake stopped in mid-flight and wheeled around. "That's why everyone in town knows our personal business," he complained. "Everyone thinks we're gettin' divorced."

"We *are* getting divorced, Jake," she replied coolly.

"Ain't that why we're here? We're tryin' to patch things up, right? Ain't that what this guy's gonna do?"

She didn't say anything. We reached the office and they sat in the chairs I'd arranged facing the desk. Jake leaned forward, and Grace sat back and folded her arms.

"Before we talk about what you hope to accomplish here, why don't you tell me a little bit about yourselves?" I invited them.

"Like what?" Jake asked.

"What you do for a living, for starters."

"I'm a secretary at Jackson and Harris," Grace mentioned the name of a local law firm. "I've been there eleven years."

"What about you, Jake?"

"They call me the breeder man," he said.

I gathered that he wanted me to press him for an explanation. "Does that mean you raise chickens or you have a lot of kids?"

"Means I'm an A.I. tech."

"What exactly does an A.I. tech do?"

"Artificial insemination," he educated me. "I go around to farms with frozen bull sperm in liquid nitrogen, and I get the cows pregnant."

"Sounds like a tough job."

"Not long as you don't mind stickin' your arm up a cow's uterus while she's in heat."

"That would eliminate a lot of people right there, including me."

"Buddy, it's the future. Farmers don't have to keep bulls no more. I can knock up a cow good as any bull can."

"I don't doubt it."

"Pay's good, too."

I turned back to Grace. "It sounds like you and Jake go off to completely different worlds every day."

"I'm with the business crowd and he's with the farmers. That's the problem. We don't have anything in common."

"Bullshit, Grace!" Jake nearly came out of his chair. "We fit together when we got married! We still fit together!"

"We were eighteen Jake. We hardly knew each other."

"Let's talk about what you have in common," I interjected. "What are some of your shared interests?"

"We don't have any," Grace said.

"Hell if we don't. We're both Steelers' fans."

"You're the Steelers' fan," Grace said. "I don't care if they win or lose."

His mouth fell open. "Then how come you got autographed pictures of Terry Bradshaw and Franco Harris hangin' in your office?"

"Because you gave them to me for Valentine's Day," she refreshed his memory.

"You love football and you know it."

"Okay, maybe Jake's a little more into the Steelers," I summed it up. "What else do you like to do together?"

"Mud boggin'," Jake said. "We got this ol' jacked-up Chivvy truck runs like a scalded puppy. We take 'er down to Monroe County and make the Fords eat our mud."

"And you both enjoy doing this?"

Grace rolled her eyes and made a pained face.

"I saw that, Grace! You'n me both love mud boggin' and you know it."

"Jake, I'm tired of spending Saturday nights scrubbing the mud off 48-inch tires."

"Well hon, you know we can't be leavin' them tars like that."

I stepped in again. "Grace, what would you rather be doing?"

"Going out to dinner. Going to the movies."

"Borin'."

"You're just hyper, Jake," she said. "You've always got to be doing something."

"Doin' somethin's better'n doin' nothin'."

They continued bickering back and forth. Jake was a cold Bud, Grace a glass of Chardonnay. "Do you have any children?" I asked them.

"Nope," Jake said. "We got medical problems."

"You have the medical problem," Grace corrected him.

"Well, hon, how do we know that?"

"It's your sperm count, Jake."

"Maybe there's somethin' wrong with your plumbin', too. We don't know."

"There's definitely something wrong with yours."

"The Lord just don't want us to have kids."

"Maybe He knows we're getting divorced."

"God you're a pig-headed woman." He turned to me. "Ain't you gonna help us none?"

"What would you like me to do?"

"Talk 'er out of it."

"Do you think that's my job?"

"That's what you're getting' paid for, ain't it?"

"No, that's not exactly what marriage counseling is about."

"Then what the hell is it about?"

I made appointments to see them separately.

I thought Grace would be more relaxed one-on-one, but she seemed nervous. A few minutes into our conversation she let the cat out of the bag. "I should probably tell you something," she said. "I didn't bring it up before because Jake doesn't know about it."

"That's why I'm meeting with you privately."

"I'm having an affair with Mark Harris."

"Your boss?"

She nodded.

"What's Mark's marital status?"

"He's leaving his wife so we can be together."

"Are you sure?"

"Yes."

"Jake doesn't know about it?"

She shook her head.

"When are you planning to tell him?"

"I'm not."

"You're not going to tell him why you're leaving him?"

"He'd kill Mark!"

"You really think so?"

She started to say yes, but the wind went out of her sails. "Not really. Jake likes to pretend he's this big macho guy, but he's really just a teddy bear. He depends on me for everything. I don't think he's ever been with another woman. He probably thinks if we get divorced no one else will want him."

"Grace, if you leave Jake and turn around and marry your boss, it's not going to be that hard for him to put two-and-two together. Aren't you better off telling him now? He thinks you're leaving him because you're tired of mud bogging."

"I am tired of it."

"I understand that, but you need to be honest with Jake. It's not going to be pleasant, but you can only put it off for so long. We can talk about other things, but in the end you're going to have to face the fact that you're having an affair."

She looked pensive. "Do you really think I should tell him?"

I didn't like to tell clients what to do; the answers needed to come from them. "I'm not sure if it's the best thing," I leveled with her.

"You'll have to decide that. I don't know the personalities involved. But it just seems to me you're not being fair to Jake."

She didn't say anything. I'd given her too much to think about.

A few days later it was Jake's turn. He plopped down in the chair and got right to the point. "Guess you know the damn bitch was foolin' round on me. I got me a lawyer and I'm suin' her ass."

"How did you feel when she told you?"

"Now, buddy, there's a dumbass question. How would you feel your wife done you like that?"

"Not so great."

"Damn straight. I trusted the stupid bitch! Twelve fuckin' years down the toilet."

"So you want the divorce now?"

"Hell, yeah. The quicker the better. And I'll tell you sumpin' else," he said, shaking a finger at me. "If she thinks she's gettin' the truck, she's got another thought comin'."

I gave up on the idea of seeing them together again. I wanted to ask Grace if she'd had a conversation with Mark Harris, and how it had gone. I found her in the waiting room. She looked glum for someone who was supposed to be on the verge of an exciting new life. She trudged up the stairs like she was carrying the weight of the world on her shoulders.

When we reached the office I asked if she was okay.

"No." she said. "Jake called me a slut."

"Did you talk with Mark?"

Her eyes brimmed with tears. "Yes. He said he thinks it's better if we don't see each other any more. He said he'd help me find another job." The tears began to flow like miniature waterfalls.

I gave her a tissue. "That's one reason you needed to have this conversation with him, Grace. Guys who fool around on their wives aren't always 100% trustworthy."

"I should have talked with him before I told Jake. I did it the other way around. Now I feel like a fool."

"I guess the one positive thing that's come out of all this is that now Jake's willing to go ahead with the divorce."

"I don't want a divorce!" she blubbered.

I beat a hasty retreat to Anne Blair's office. "I'm not cut out for marriage counseling," I tried to convince her. "I'm totally screwing up this case. Isn't there someone who can step in and take over?"

"Margo's excellent," she said.

"Margo's in Switzerland," I reminded her of our latest postcard. "I'm not qualified to do marriage counseling. At first this lady wanted a divorce and he didn't. Now after my expert intervention, he wants one and she doesn't. She took my advice and she lost her job."

"Affair with the boss?" she guessed.

"Yeah. But does it sound to you like I'm doing a good job?"

"These things might have happened anyway," she reminded me.

"What am I going to do for these people?"

"Marriage counseling has never been our strong suit," she admitted. "We don't have anybody who likes doing it except Margo. We can hold hands after marriages fall apart, but we're not very good at saving them."

"Have you thought about adding someone to the staff who is?"

She lit a cigarette. Anne Blair always seemed to think better when she smoked, like the answers were floating somewhere in the cloud above her desk. "There's an Episcopal priest at the church up the street who's looking for part-time work," she said. "He's willing to come in for a couple of hours in the evenings. He'd be perfect. But we don't have the money to hire him."

"That's never stopped you before."

"I'm trying to kick the habit."

"Maybe you should work on cigarettes instead," I suggested, eying the Himalayan pile of butts in her ashtray. "This is really important, Anne Blair. The clinic needs a marriage counselor."

"You're right," she admitted, half-irritated and half-amused. "I don't know if you're the angel on my right shoulder or the devil on my left."

"I'm the angel. The devil wouldn't tell you to hire a priest."

Father Andy was a noisy, joyous presence. He was in his mid-thirties and his hair was going the way of Friar Tuck's, and he had a little extra padding from too many church suppers. He'd walk into the clinic singing and greeting everyone. His voice had natural projection, and I wondered if we were going to be able to hear his sessions through the walls. (When I was in Catholic school we had an elderly priest who was hard of hearing. When you stood in line with your classmates waiting to make your confession, you could hear his voice booming from the confessional booth. *You did what! How many times? With yourself or with others?"* Your poor classmate would emerge red-faced. It was the equivalent of a public flogging.)

I caught Father Andy writing up case notes after his first meeting with Jake and Grace. I plopped down in his office. "I know the Garlands aren't my case now, but how are they doing?"

"I think they'll make it," he predicted. "They're both wrapped up in themselves and they need to pay more attention to each other, but I'm sure you noticed that."

"Yeah, I noticed it. I just didn't know what to do about it."

"Marriage counseling isn't like crisis work," he said. "Relationships are long-term projects. I'll probably be working with these folks at least two or three months." He raised a triumphant fist. "Yes! Job security!"

"I guess you're happily married, huh?" I asked him.

"I've got to be. We can't afford a divorce."

"So what 's the secret to being a good marriage counselor?"

"Love of gossip. But it's a drag - you hear all this great dirt about people and you can't tell anyone." He grew serious. "There's something I want to ask you, but it needs to stay between us. Okay?"

"Sure."

"Anne Blair made a passing comment about finding the money to pay me. She sounded a little iffy. I'd love to be able to donate my services, but my wife works part-time and we're raising two children. I'm trying to supplement our income." He studied me hopefully. "She wouldn't have hired me if she didn't have the money, would she?"

"O ye of little faith."

"Oh, shit."

You had to love a preacher who cussed.

Chapter 11
Born on a Roller Coaster

Folks in the Greenbrier Valley have a fond spot in their hearts for the West Virginia State Fair, which runs for nine days every August on a permanent fairground just south of Lewisburg. A few of the locals grumble about the traffic, but their complaints are drowned by the majority, who look forward to the rides, competitions, livestock sales and calories.

As I watched my first State Fair coming to life I was impressed by how much work it took to throw this annual shindig. A tribe of grungy nomads had rolled into town, and they were busy bolting together Round-Ups, Tilt-a-Whirls, Pirate Ships and Ferris Wheels. Concessionaires were airing out their stands and firing up their grills. Exhibitors were delivering quilts, veggies and elaborately decorated cakes to the West Virginia Building. Craftspeople were arranging their leatherwork and pottery and stained glass. Draft horses were taking up residence in barns and lop-eared bunnies were looking adorable in their hutches.

Hank was the clinic's point man during fair week. Alcohol was banned on the fairgrounds, but some hardcore revelers considered the State Fair a place where the usual laws didn't apply, like Woodstock. State troopers were determined to convince them otherwise. They didn't want to waste jail space on these party animals, so they rounded them up and delivered them to Hank on the theory that they needed treatment. Most of them thought they just needed another drink. Hank had his hands full.

Jack McManus, a counselor with the local branch of the state's Vocational Rehabilitation division, dropped by my office. "I think one of my clients is about to run off with the carnival," he said. "I went to his house this morning to take him to Institute for six months of janitorial training and he wasn't there. His mother says he's hanging around the carnival and he's planning to leave town with them."

"He's just getting a different kind of vocational training, Jack," I reacted. "The world needs carnies, too."

"This kid's way too naïve for that kind of life. He's got a 78 IQ."

"What do you want me to do?"

"Play detective," he requested. "Go over to the fair and see if you can find him. If he sees me coming he'll take off because I'm the guy who wants to send him away for training. See if you can figure out what's going on with him."

"How will I recognize him?"

He opened the file folder he'd brought along and showed me a picture. "He's eighteen. He's a little guy, and he has sandy blonde hair and blue eyes. He usually needs a haircut and he's got a scraggly little goat beard that won't grow."

I took the photo. "He looks like a Keebler elf."

"He's a little funny-turned,' he warned me. "He wears plaid and stripes, stuff that doesn't go together. He's one of a kind."

"Maybe he's got a natural fashion sense that you and I obviously lack. What's his name?"

"Medwin Bales."

"Medwin?"

"Medwin. He's from a single parent home and his mother's a little funny-turned herself. The apple doesn't fall too far from the tree."

"You're right," I agreed. "When it does, it usually rolls downhill."

I decided to take in the fair before I went searching for Medwin. I started at the livestock arena, where some Future Farmers were showing their pigs. These porky lovelies weren't exactly striking poses like the dogs at Westminster. Pigs were scurrying every which way, ignoring the energetic thwacks they were receiving on their thick hides from flyswatters-type switches designed to steer them. In the middle of all this porcine chaos, ribbons were passed out and the ring was cleared for the next stampede. I noticed that some of the young women were frilled up like they were the contestants and the pigs were their accessories. Still, you had to admire a girl who could handle a three hundred pound pig – it was great preparation for boyfriends and husbands.

I left the livestock arena and headed over to the midway to find Medwin. I ran into our business manager Corny and his wife Cindy. He was carrying a grease-stained sack full of donuts and they were eating them. "Have you tried the Ben-Ellen donuts?" he asked me.

"No, I haven't," I said. "My heart belongs to Krispy Kreme."

"Ben-Ellen donuts are better than Krispy Kreme," he made an outrageous claim. "They're better than sex. You're not a resident of the Greenbrier Valley until you've scarfed down a dozen of these babies."

"Where do you get them?" He pointed to a concession stand by the grandstand, where four long lines of fairgoers were waiting. "Are Ben and Ellen your parents, Corny? Is that why you're pushing these things? Is this your family's business?"

"I wish. If you're ever on Death Row you'll request Ben-Ellen donuts for your last meal."

"Okay, okay," I fell for his hard sell. I went over and joined one of the queues. The customers looked like junkies shuffling into a methadone clinic. As I drew closer to the counter I saw little golden cakes dropping from the baking machines. The young women behind the counter dredged them through sugar and cinnamon, strung them on wooden sticks and slid them into bags.

When it was my turn I asked the counter girl a question. "Should I eat them now or will they keep?"

The granny in sneakers behind me gasped. "Oh, you must eat them now! They're so much better when they're hot!"

I bought two donuts, found a place to sit down and took my first bite. The golden crust crunched lightly, giving way to a waterfall of sugar, cake and grease. I imagined my arteries clogging like a drain, but I inhaled them and got back in line.

A few donuts later I went looking for Medwin. I didn't have to go far; he was standing at the entrance to the midway. He was wearing a T-shirt and a leopard print vest and manning a strength-testing machine, the kind where you whack a target to ring a bell. He didn't have a carnie personality; he wasn't hawking his attraction or chatting it up with his marks. He assisted passively, accepting tickets, handing over the rubber mallet, and rewarding the bell ringers with chintzy prizes. I'd heard that some of these games were rigged, but at first glance the Strength-O-Meter seemed to work as advertised. Brawny guys rang the bell and kids limped into the Try Again zone, forked over another ticket and took another whack. But as I continued to watch from a discrete distance, I noticed that fairly regularly someone who looked like they had the right stuff couldn't make it. They were determined repeaters, bent on rescuing their wounded pride. About the time they looked ready to stomp off in frustration they rang the bell. But how would you rig something like this? I waited for business to die down and I strolled over.

"How many tickets?" I asked him.

He pointed to a sign that read ONE TICKET in big letters. I forked over a ticket and he gave me the mallet. I reared back and gave it my all, which wasn't enough. I took another shot and again fell short. The third time I watched Medwin. I noticed he was standing on an innocent-looking cord that looked like an electrical extension. "Could you step back? You're making me nervous."

"I have to stand here," he insisted.

"How come?"

"It's my job."

"It's your job to stand on that cord?"

He smiled sheepishly.

"Step back for just a second."

He complied, and I clobbered the target and rang the bell.

He rewarded me with a plastic back-scratcher.

"Keep it," I said. "Give it to someone who can't ring the bell."

I could see Medwin wasn't a conversationalist, but I tried to chat him up anyway. "Does this job pay pretty good?"

"Ten dollars."

The minimum wage at the time was $2.30, so I figured he was making ten dollars a day, not ten dollars an hour.

"What time do you start?"

"Nine-thirty."

"What time do you get off?"

"Closing."

The fair ran until midnight, which meant he was working 14 hours for ten bucks. "Do you get lunch and dinner breaks?"

He shook his head.

"How do you eat?"

"They bring me food sometimes."

I suspected that behind this *Oliver Twist* work arrangement, some carnie version of Fagin was pulling the strings. "Will you leave town when the carnival does?"

He nodded proudly. "Yep, me 'n Johnny Cash."

"I don't think Johnny travels with the carnival," I tried to set him straight. "Just because he's playing here doesn't mean he works for them."

"Yes he does," he insisted. "They said so."

I could see this was going to take some time. "I'll be back tomorrow to try my luck again," I promised him.

"I won't stand on the cord," he offered magnanimously.

"Thanks. I'm Greg. What's your name?"

"Medwin."

"I'll bring you a present tomorrow, Medwin."

"What?"

"You'll have to wait and see."

The next evening as I was leaving my trailer an all-too familiar voice called from across the street. "Are you going to the fair?"

Millie was standing on her porch. She still hadn't given up the notion that I was boyfriend material, even though I was trying my best to discourage her. "Yeah."

"If you don't have any plans, maybe we could go together," she suggested.

I didn't want to tell her I'd rather have a root canal. Fortunately I had a ready excuse. "I'm working at the fair," I said.

She eyed me skeptically. "You're working at the State Fair?"

"I've got to meet a guy there. It's related to my job at the clinic." I could see she wasn't buying it. "Why don't you go with Ginny?"

"Ginny's going with her friends. I don't want to hang around with a bunch of high school kids. I'm too mature for that crowd."

"Then I guess I'm immature," I said. "I like high school kids." I hopped in my Jeep and drove off, leaving her to continue pondering the riddle of the strange guy across the street.

The Strength-O-Meter was a minor attraction that needed to be pitched to fairgoers as they walked over to the rides. Medwin wasn't a pitchman. At the rate his carnival career was going, pretty soon he'd be reassigned to mop up vomit on the Round Up.

People with IQs in the 70's and low 80's tend to think concretely, which doesn't help in academics, where abstract thought is rewarded. Statistically, about 7% of the population tests at this level, with another 2-3% scoring lower than 70 and classifying as mentally impaired. It's interesting to think that 10% of our citizens struggle to understand the contracts they sign, their tax obligations, or how right-of-way works in driving. We take it for granted that just about everyone can grasp these things when millions can't. I knew I needed to keep things simple for Medwin.

"How's business?" I asked as he stood with his mallet, waiting for customers who weren't there.

"Bad."

"Why don't you take a break for a few minutes, Medwin? Come with me and I'll give you the present I was telling you about."

"I can't leave."

"Why not?"

"It's my job."

"What do you do when you have to use the restroom?"

He pointed to the West Virginia Building. "I go over there."

"Who watches the Strength-O-Meter while you're gone?"

"Nobody."

"If you can leave long enough to go to the restroom, you can come with me for a couple of minutes."

"Where are we going?"

"Just down to the other end of the grandstand." He left the Strength-O-Meter and followed me to the Ben-Ellen stand. "Have you ever tried these?"

He shook his head.

"I'll get six for you and six for me."

"I can't eat six."

"I'll get a dozen and you can eat however many you want."

The scene at the stand looked like the day before, with a crush of people waiting. When Medwin sampled his first donut, it was love at first bite. He inhaled his half of our supply with sugar collecting on his vest. I noticed he was wearing the same clothes as the day before.

"You ought to talk with these folks about a job, Medwin," I encouraged him as he munched away. "You're not even making a dollar an hour now. I'm sure this place pays better. And you won't have to stand around waiting for customers. They stay busy all the time."

I'd already spoken with the manager, who had agreed to give him a trial.

"But I won't get to meet Johnny Cash," he objected. "He doesn't work for these donut people."

"He doesn't work for the carnival either," I tried to convince him. "He'll pull up behind the stage in his tour bus. He'll do his show and maybe sign a few autographs. Then he'll leave and go on to the next town he's playing. That's what all these performers do. They work for themselves. If you're here at the donut stand you'll be closer to the stage and you can hear the concert. If you're at the carnival you won't be able to hear him over the noise from the rides."

"I like the carnival," he protested. "I was born on a roller coaster."

"Really?"

"Uh huh. Mama says so."

"Your mother gave birth on a roller coaster?"

"Yeah."

"She sounds like an interesting person."

He smiled, but I didn't know if it was because he was pulling my leg or because I thought his mother was interesting.

"They're taking advantage of you at the Strength-O-Meter, Medwin. With all your hours and overtime you should be making $40 a day. They're cheating you, and they're teaching you to cheat the customers. Let's go around back and talk to the manager here, okay?"

"Okay."

We found the entrepreneur rolling in dough – he was stuffing currency in bank deposit pouches. When I'd spoken to him earlier he was rolling in the other kind, mixing his secret ingredients by hand. I left Medwin for his interview and told him I'd be back in ten or fifteen minutes. I'd discovered that the Ben-Ellen family was part of the local community, and that they also owned a greenhouse and lawn mowing service. I knew Medwin would be in good hands.

I strolled back over to the midway. A short, plump man was standing by the Strength-O-Meter looking irritated. Fagin, I gathered.

"Are you looking for the boy who was here?" I asked him.

"Yeah. You seen the little dimwit?"

"There was a guy here a few minutes ago from the West Virginia Division of Weights and Measures. He was asking him a lot of questions. I think he got scared and took off."

His brow furrowed. "What the hell's the Division of Weights and Measures?"

"Aren't they the people who inspect gas pumps?"

He bent down with some effort, yanked out the cord that controlled the machine, and stuffed it in his pocket. "Thanks, buddy," he said. He dashed off.

I went back for Medwin.

"He said I can have all the donuts I want," he reported the highlight of his interview.

"When can you start?"

"Now."

"Good. I guess I'll see you whenever I stop by."

The fair parking lot sprawled across a large field on the opposite side of Route 219. As I searched for my Jeep I could look over and see the blaze of lights and hear the cacophony of noise and music. A small roller coaster sat at the far end of the fairground. The Medwin Bales Birthplace, no doubt.

Chapter 12
River Rats

My work life was going well, but my social life was nothing to write home about. I was spending most of my time being a rookie social worker and volunteer firefighter. I had some things in common with the guys at the firehouse, but we had our differences, too. I read fiction and nonfiction and tried to keep up with the news and politics, and most of the other firefighters were more hands-on and not especially interested in these things. We talked some about WVU football, but the 1970's weren't exactly the Mountaineers' golden era. We lost Bobby Bowden to Florida State, for example.

I hadn't dated anyone since I'd left the university. A couple of young women had tried to strike up relationships, but they weren't my type. I imagined my type: olive skin, long black hair, educated, adventurous, artsy. I'd seen someone who looked like this in a Camels' ad. She was standing at an easel, painting and ignoring her boyfriend's smoking habit. I got a little fixated on her, which probably wasn't a good sign.

Millie was still keeping track of my comings and goings from her upstairs window. Ginny told me that her sister had decided that I was gay; she was trying to catch me sneaking in a boyfriend. She was still unemployed and growing unhappier by the day. Anne Blair could have worked wonders with her, but I wasn't about to suggest to Millie that she needed a therapist.

She was standing in my yard one evening, complaining about how much Alderson sucked, when a young woman came running around the corner and jogged past us. She had long, flowing golden hair. She looked like an angel in running shorts. My eyes followed her up the street. "Who's that?" I asked Millie.

"Libby Meadows."

"Who is she? I haven't seen her before."

"Just some college girl," she said dismissively.

"Does she live here?"

"I don't know where she lives," she said with irritation. "I don't hang around with people like that."

It was a ringing endorsement.

Our movement therapist Penelope caught me in the hallway between appointments. "I'm getting some people together to go rafting on the New River on Saturday," she said. "It's less expensive if you've got six. We need one more. Are you interested?"

"I've never been on serious white water before," I told her.

"There's nothing to it. We'll be in a 16-foot inflatable raft, with a river guide in back steering with oars. Everyone has a paddle and the guide tells you what to do. We're running the lower section of the New, the part with class IV and V rapids."

"How much does it cost?"

"Forty dollars."

"Forty dollars each?"

"Don't be such a cheapskate," she chided me. "It seems like a lot, but you get six hours on the river and they stop and feed you lunch. It's a fourteen-mile trip."

A young entrepreneur named Jon Dragan had launched the rafting industry in the New River Gorge in 1969. Other companies quickly sprang up, and people were coming from all over the country for the adventure. Most of the rafting companies offered two trips on the New, the Upper or Lower sections. The Upper was a gentle ride, with long stretches of quiet water and a few mild rapids for a little excitement. It was popular with first-timers and families with children. The Lower was a roller coaster ride through a narrow gorge, with giant boulders, bouncy holes and twenty-five named rapids. There was some danger on the Lower, and every year or so you'd hear about someone who'd fallen out of a raft and drowned, but thousands had run it successfully and come back for more. The odds were with you.

"Okay, count me in," I decided to go for it. "When and where?"

"We're meeting at the post office parking lot at 6:30 Saturday morning and riding together. It takes a couple of hours to get there. Wear a swimsuit and a T-shirt, and bring a cap. The sun really beats down on you."

"I'll be there," I promised her.

We were standing in front of the firehouse after our weekly drill when the angel jogged past us. All eyes followed her as she crossed the old bridge that connected the Monroe and Greenbrier sides of town. "Who's that?" I asked, wanting a better version than Millie's.

"Libby Meadows," my friend Randy said. "Her dad's a carpenter and her mom teaches at the high school. She just finished college. She's been making pottery."

"You seem to know a lot about her," I couldn't help noticing.

He gave me a sly grin. "I'm thinking about asking her out. I was wondering if I could borrow your Jeep on Saturday so I can take her up on Keeney's Knob?"

I felt a little jealous, and I had a ready excuse. "Sorry, Randy. I need my Jeep on Saturday. I'm meeting some people and we're going white water rafting."

"How about Sunday?"

"What if I need to go somewhere?"

"You can use my Camero. I'll come by your place and we'll swap."

Randy loved his Camero, and this was probably the first time he'd offered to let someone else drive it. This little outing apparently meant a lot to him. "Okay," I agreed. "But what if I wreck it?"

He shrugged it off. "I've got insurance."

On Saturday morning I climbed in a VW Microbus and rode over to Fayette County with Penelope and four of her friends. They were back-to-the-earth types who'd moved to West Virginia in search of a rural lifestyle. There were pockets of these homesteaders throughout the valley. They would eventually become an integral part of the community, but they socialized with each other and considered themselves a counterculture, so they had yet to be assimilated. Some of them cultivated marijuana, which didn't exactly endear them to law enforcement and the courts. The locals called them hippies, but the hippie era had pretty much passed. As the years went on most of these homesteaders would give up subsistence farming and become business owners, teachers and artisans. Their children would grow up as West Virginia natives, and the assimilation would be complete.

The conversation was spirited, but when it turned to environmental issues I grew uncharacteristically quiet. They were of the mind that the best development was no development, and that highway construction, housing developments and power lines were a rape of the land. They viewed their adopted home as a pristine land best left untouched by the hand of man. I had somewhat different views, but I didn't want to argue.

The rafting company's headquarters was buzzing with activity. Cars with out-of-state license plates filled the parking lot. People were lathering up with sunscreen, donning wetsuits and floppy hats, and bickering about what they should or shouldn't take along on the trip.

"Leave your camera in the car, Gina," one father sternly ordered his young daughter.

"But, Daddy, I want pictures to show my friends," she protested.

"You're going to get soaked," her mother explained. "Your camera's not waterproof. They've got photographers who take pictures at some of the rapids. We can buy one when we get back."

"Promise?"

"No," her father said. "If you can't see our faces I'm not spending ten bucks for a picture."

It was obvious from the large number of people milling around that rafting had become an operatic-scale enterprise. Half a dozen companies would be running the New River that morning. An inflatable fleet carrying hundreds of people would be snaking its way downriver. They herded us onto a school bus and shuttled us to our put-in spot in the hamlet of Thurmond, an old railroad town memorialized in *Ripley's Believe It or Not* for hosting the world's longest running poker game - 14 years. Once home to 500 hardy souls, Thurmond's population had dwindled to 10.

Penelope was an enthusiastic feminist, so she was pleased to learn that our guide was a woman. She was heavily muscled; she looked like she could hitch a rope to a truck and pull it uphill. She introduced herself to us as Cheyenne the River Goddess. Cheyenne made sure we had our life vests and helmets, and she partnered us with someone who sat on the opposite side of the raft. Cheyenne took her place in back, steering the raft with the kind of giant oars you saw in pictures of old Nantucket lifesaving boats. I was sitting in the middle on the left. My partner, Rob, was a bushy-bearded guy who told me he was trying to make a living off beekeeping and tapping maple trees. "Honey and syrup don't have to get inspected by the USDA because they're 100% natural," he informed me. I was tempted to ask if he was making a living from his efforts, but I didn't want to put him on the spot in case he was supplementing his income by selling a little Mary Jane on the side. He seemed to like products that weren't government-inspected.

At first the water was calm and the ride was slow. We were making our way through long pools and silvery ripples. Red-tailed hawks flew in lazy circles above us. We had launched in the bottom stretch of the Upper New, eight miles above the rugged canyon where the river starts tumbling and dropping precipitously. "We've got perfect conditions today," Cheyenne informed us. "The gauge is reading two feet at Fayette Station."

"What does that mean?" I asked her.

"If it's at ten feet the rocks are too far under water and you lose the whitewater effect," she explained. "When it's up to twelve feet the current's too fast and we can't run it."

"What if it's below two feet?" Rob asked her.

"It's too slow. If you get trapped under a boulder there might not be enough force to push you on downstream."

"That doesn't sound good," Penelope reacted.

"Don't worry about it," Cheyenne said as she kept rowing forcefully. "The bigger the raft, the more stable the ride. A 16-footer with seven people is more stable than a 14-footer with five people. A 12-footer's like a bucking bronco. You're going to get flipped out."

"Have you tried the different sizes?" someone asked her.

"Yeah, I've even taken a kayak down the Gauley. They don't let just anybody guide. You've got to have experience."

"That's comforting to know," Penelope's friend Marta said.

Everyone was pulling his or her own weight and we were establishing our rhythm. We were a mellow crew. We weren't bickering like some of the folks we heard in the other rafts. As we moved along Cheyenne warned us about the dangers we could face up ahead. They included keeper holes that trap you in circular motions, and pin rocks that hold you against or under them. She stressed that the last 6 or 8 miles would be the most challenging. "Don't work too hard now," she advised us. "Save your energy for after lunch."

We shot through Class III and IV rapids with fanciful names like Surprise, Piece of Cake and Lolligag. We reached what Cheyenne called a "swimmer's rapid". She invited us to slip out of the raft and float down the river on our backs feet-first, letting the current carry us along, and everyone did.

We pulled over to a large boulder called Jump Rock and played around, scrambling up on it and jumping into the river. Jump Rock was situated in an eddy near the bank and there wasn't any danger of being swept downstream by the current, which we could see flowing swiftly twenty or thirty feet away.

After a lunch of grilled burgers we took on a heart-pounding Class V rapid called the Double Z, which was exactly what it sounded like – a zigzagging course around a series of giant boulders. Despite our furious paddling we were heading straight for one of the rocks, and before we knew what was happening we'd hit it. The raft turned on its side and I flipped out. Before I knew what was happening I was underwater, trapped under the rock by the powerful current, and totally helpless. The river was going to have its way with me.

Fortunately what it decided to do was to flush me out and send me downstream. I popped up fifty feet in front of our raft and gasped for air. My helmet was missing, ripped off by the current. My teammates had gotten back on track, but I'd beaten them through the Double Z. They reached the calmer water below the rapid and pulled me back into the raft. Cheyenne looked shaken. Guides aren't supposed to look shaken. Her coworkers were piloting other rafts and had witnessed the accident. This meant she couldn't avoid reporting it to her supervisor.

"I guess Sunday's headline won't read *Social Worker Perishes in River* after all," Penelope reacted with a little gallows humor.

"I'm really glad you invited me to come along on this trip, Penelope," I said. I remembered Cheyenne's observations about the river levels. "So if the river was running low, I might not have come out from under that boulder?" I asked pointedly. She didn't reply. Later on I would read about fatalities where the same accident happened in the same spot, but the river level was lower. A teacher from New York was trapped in the Double Z for two days before rescuers could retrieve her body.

We didn't have time to think about what had just happened because we still had Class III, IV and V rapids ahead. The Greyhound Bus Stopper tried its best to suck us into a giant whirlpool, but we dug in harder and managed to skirt it. Near the end of our ride we passed under the state's best-known construction project, the New River Gorge Bridge, which at nearly 900 feet would become the highest vehicular bridge in the United States. We pulled out at Fayette Station and posed for a picture with our paddles held high in the air. The trip had been exhilarating but a little hairy.

On the way back Penelope told us that when she was changing her clothes in the locker room she'd overheard Cheyenne in the next aisle grousing to someone. Her supervisor had dressed her down for the accident. "I told him I had a weak crew!" she complained. "He said it was no excuse and I should have been able to control the raft! What can you do with a weak crew?"

"A weak crew!" we all reacted. There weren't any weaklings in our party. We were all in our twenties and thirties and in decent physical shape.

Rob put it best. "She's just trying to save her own ass by blaming the victims."

The owner of the company called Penelope the next day and offered us another trip to compensate for the incident. She told him we might take him up on it, but the next time we didn't want Cheyenne the River Goddess as our guide.

Randy came by the trailer to return my Jeep and pick up his Camero. "How did your 4-wheeling go?" I asked him.

"It was great," he said, looking pleased. "Libby really liked your Jeep. We don't have much in common but we get along fine."

"Good," I said, meaning it was good that she liked my Jeep and they didn't have much in common.

Chapter 13
The Other Side of the Desk

In the 1970's Concord College, which became Concord University in 2004, was the closest school to the Greenbrier Valley that had a social work program. Anne Blair had expressed interest in using Concord social work interns at the clinic. The idea appealed to her for two reasons: she liked having young people around, and it meant that for a relatively small outlay the clinic would have an extra pair of helping hands each semester. Since I was the only master's level social worker on the staff this meant I would have to supervise them, a chore the college called field instruction. I liked the idea, so Anne Blair invited the chairman of the Social Work program to visit the clinic. Buford Young was pleased to learn that we were willing to pay our interns; some of the agencies that took them expected them to volunteer their services. As our conversation wound down we agreed to start taking a social work student each semester, beginning in the spring.

Before he left Buford threw me a curve ball. "How would you like to teach a class for us this fall?" he proposed. "It's a class about the field of corrections."

I had imagined myself eventually teaching. I like the challenge of trying to break down complicated subjects so people can readily understand them. I'm a simple guy, and once I manage to get something through my thick skull, I can usually find a way to explain it to others. But I was recently out of graduate school and I didn't exactly have much professional experience to share with students, especially about the field of corrections. "I don't know," I hedged. "I don't think I'm ready for it yet."

"We're desperate," Buford leveled with me. "The probation officer who was going to teach it for us is moving away because her husband got transferred. We really need someone to teach this class. Sixteen students signed up for it. They need the credit hours."

"I'm not qualified to teach corrections," I said.

"Do you have an MSW degree?"

"Yes."

"Then technically you're qualified."

"But I don't know anything about the subject. Doesn't that matter?"

"Do you deal with the court system?"

"Yes, quite a bit."

"Can you follow a textbook?"

"Yes."

"Then you're my man," he anointed me. He pulled a book from his briefcase and handed it to me.

I looked at Anne Blair. "Did you know he was going to ask me to do this?"

"Buford asked me if I thought you could handle it and I said yes," she admitted. "I told him you were a quick study."

"The guys in the Alderson Fire Department don't think I'm a quick study. I still can't figure out how to drive the fire engine."

"You won't have to drive any fire engines at Concord," he promised.

"I could use the extra money," I gave it more consideration. "When does the class start?"

"The day after Labor Day," Buford said. "It meets on Tuesday and Thursday nights."

"That's next week."

"Greg, I hope you understand this isn't how we usually operate. We were counting on this woman and she bailed on us at the last minute. If you teach this semester and you like it, we'll offer you some other classes. It'll give you a way to get your foot in the door in case you ever want to apply for a full-time position." He looked at Anne Blair and realized he was sounding like a recruiter. "I'm not talking about anytime soon," he added hastily. "I'm talking down the road."

"What would my title be?"

"Adjunct professor."

I liked the professor part. Adjunct suggested the program couldn't afford to add another full-time faculty member and was making do with a part-timer who didn't require benefits. Still something about it appealed to me. "Okay, I'm in," I signed on.

The words *adjunct professor* brought up an experience at West Virginia University that I still hadn't been able to get out of my mind. All the social work faculty were full-time except Carl Mullins, who worked for the VA in Clarksburg and drove to Morgantown once a week to teach Human Behavior in the Social Environment. Carl was an overweight, ashen-faced, joyless man who had "career bureaucrat" written all over him. He wasn't a good teacher and he could make even interesting subjects boring. But HBSE was a required course and I needed it. I slogged unenthusiastically through the work.

At the end of the semester Carl did something totally unexpected. In addition to taking a final exam he assigned us to write a two-page paper on how we planned to practice social work. It was due the week before the class ended, and he didn't give us any guidelines for the paper.

For some reason this little assignment fired my imagination. It made me think about where I hoped my life would lead. I wrote and refined, wrote and polished. Three days later I'd produced seven pages, written in the form of a letter to my professor. I opened by explaining that he needed to know something about my past to understand my future hopes. I reviewed some of the experiences that led me to choose a social work career, and then sketched out the things I wanted to do. I divided the document into four sections, and I used the lyrics from popular songs at the beginning of each section. When I handed in the finished product, I realized I didn't even care if he read it; I'd written it entirely for my own benefit.

When we finished our final exam he gave our papers back, wished us luck and sent us on our way. As I started to leave the room he asked me to stay for a few minutes. Ordinarily I wouldn't have minded this, but I had some pressing business. Two close friends, Patrick and Karin Heffernan, who lived three hours away in the Eastern Panhandle town of Moorefield, were moving to Cambridge, England. I'd promised to drive them to Dulles airport so they could catch their transatlantic flight, which left at seven that evening. I planned to leave my dog at their house, then come back and spend the night before heading back to Morgantown.

In addition to friends who were waiting for a ride to Dulles airport, I had a nervous sheepdog waiting in the parking lot at the Coliseum, where the class was held. I tried to explain to my professor that I needed to go, but something about my paper had moved him to want to share all his problems with me. As I stood in the classroom, trying not to look too antsy, he told me about his battle with depression and his pending divorce. I nodded sympathetically as he explained how much he hated his federal job but felt trapped in it because of the generous health and retirement benefits. He went on with a litany of woes that made Job seem carefree by comparison. I only half-listened - all I could think about were my friends and my poor dog. He rambled on and on, and a half-hour crawled by before I managed to mumble some banalities and make my escape.

As I returned to my vehicle I felt a sense of relief that was short-lived. Alfie had grown anxious waiting for me, and his anxiety had taken the form of an attack of diarrhea. Without going into much detail, let's just say that there are few canine messes worse than an Old English Sheepdog with diarrhea. His voluminous fur coat and the interior of the Jeep were covered with smelly brown liquid. Making matters worse, I didn't have anything to wipe up the mess except ...

I ripped my masterwork apart and mopped up the damage as best I could. I deposited the sheets in a trashcan, dashed into a restroom and grabbed all the paper towels I could find. I wet some of them and went back outside to work on the situation. Twenty minutes later the Jeep looked better but poor Alfie was still a gigantic mess. I drove to a nearby carwash and gave him a bath with the spray wand. I was running seriously late, so he was going to have to air-dry on the way to Moorefield.

Miraculously we made it to the airport on time. Patrick and Karin caught their flight and lived happily in Cambridge for the next ten years. They had three sons while they were in England, who quickly Americanized when they moved back to the States.

Whenever I heard the words *adjunct professor* I thought of poor Carl and shuddered. And now, God help me, I was going to be one.

I called Buford's office.

"What's up?" he sounded worried. "You haven't changed your mind about teaching the class, have you?"

"No, but I've got a question. Do I have to use the textbook you gave me?"

"No. Is there another one you'd rather use?"

"I'd rather not use a textbook," I surprised him. "I've got an idea. Suppose every Tuesday I brought a guest speaker to class, someone who has knowledge about some aspect of the legal system or correctional system?"

"Like who?"

"A circuit court judge, a prosecuting attorney, a prison warden, a parole officer, a lawyer, a juvenile probation officer, a former prison inmate," I ticked off some the people I knew who might be willing to share their expertise with my students. "Then suppose every Thursday we reviewed what the speaker said and I helped them put it in perspective? I don't know much about corrections, but I know plenty of people who do. I think the students might find listening to real-life experiences more interesting than reading statistics about recidivism. I could even arrange for them to take a tour of the Federal Prison for Women in Alderson. I know some people who work there."

"This might take a lot more work on your part."

"I guess so, but I'd rather facilitate discussions than deliver lectures."

"You call the shots," he said. "It's called academic freedom. As long as the students learn what they're supposed to, I don't care how you do it."

"I'll read the text so I'll know what they usually cover," I promised. "Then I'll try to figure out how to turn it into a discussion format."

"Your students will be happy that they don't have to buy textbooks."

"This makes me feel better about teaching the class."

"Good. While I've got you on the phone, the department's having a little pizza party on Sunday evening. We want to give the incoming freshmen a chance to meet their professors and some of the other students. We'd like for you to come. You'll get a better picture of the program and the kind of students we have. We're meeting at five o'clock in one of the private dining rooms in the cafeteria."

"Okay, I'll be there."

"You're welcome to bring your wife."

"I don't have a wife, Buford," I said. "But maybe I can find one."

I hesitated before I picked up the phone. I dialed the number quickly; I was afraid I might change my mind and hang up. "Is Libby there?" I asked her mother. A minute later the blonde angel was on the line.

"Hi, this is Greg Johnson," I said. "You probably don't know who I am."

"You're Randy's friend with the Jeep," she surprised me. "I've seen you around. You're in the fire department and you've got a sheepdog."

"Yep, I'm the same guy. Listen, this might seem like a strange invitation, but would you like to go to a pizza party at Concord College with me on Sunday? I'm teaching part-time in their social work program and they're having a little get-together for the new students to meet the faculty. They said I could bring a guest. I thought about bringing my dog, but I'd like to make a better impression."

"So I'm standing in for your dog?"

"No. If you don't want to go, my dog's standing in for you."

She laughed. "Then maybe I'd better go."

For some reason we kept talking, and it was an easy conversation. I didn't know how Randy would feel about my calling Libby, but they weren't really an item and she wasn't saying anything to discourage me. She told me she'd graduated from West Virginia Wesleyan and had spent the past year apprenticing with a potter. She doubted that she was going to try to make a living from it; she didn't like the constant traveling around to fairs and craft shows, marketing her wares. She enjoyed making pottery, but she didn't like sales. We talked on and on. It was a rather lengthy conversation for two people who really didn't know each other.

Yet.

Chapter 14
The Night Shift

It was a day that wouldn't end. I finally made it home by nine, walked Alfie and turned into a couch potato in front of the TV. At ten o'clock the phone rang. It was Brody Allen, a small time drug dealer, recently paroled from the state's medium security prison at Huttonsville. He'd lived at our Fellowship Home for two months before his parole officer had installed him in an efficiency apartment over one of the stores in downtown Lewisburg. Brody wasn't your stereotypic ex-con. Young, angular and permanently tan, he looked deceptively All-American, like the captain of the Dartmouth tennis team. Largely because of his looks the people who had worked with him felt he had "potential". I had my doubts.

"Man, I need someone to talk to," he said.

"Okay, Brody, talk."

"Come on over to my place."

"I just got home and I'm really tired. Is this some kind of emergency?"

"Yeah, I guess you could say that."

"Can you be more specific?"

"I'm thinkin' about killin' myself. Is that an emergency?"

Two possibilities immediately came to mind. One was that he was really thinking about doing himself in. The other was that he just wanted company. I tested him with one of the questions hotlines use to determine if their callers are actively suicidal. "Have you thought about how you'd do it?" It sounded like I was asking for gory details, but people who are seriously thinking about taking their own lives have usually considered a method.

"Yeah," he said. "I'm gonna fill my bathtub with hot water, slit my wrists and bleed to death. It'll be like going to sleep."

A knife was an uncommon choice. Fifty-five percent of the men in our country who commit suicide use guns. Twenty-five percent hang themselves. Fifteen percent choose drugs or poison. But I couldn't discount what he was saying just because he was claiming he was going to use an unpopular method. One of the terms of his parole was that he wasn't supposed to have any firearms, but he had kitchen knives. "Brody, I'm curious. Why did you call me instead of just going ahead and doing it?"

"I need you to talk me out of it, man."

"Why do you want to kill yourself?"

"Life sucks."

"Tell me about it."

"Come on over."

I didn't have much choice. "Give me a few minutes. Promise me you won't do anything in the meanwhile. I don't want to get there and find you in the tub."

"Yeah, okay."

"I need something better than 'yeah, okay'."

"I said I'd wait."

"Okay. I'll see you in 20 minutes."

The speed limit on the river road was 55. I tore up it at 75 or 80, hoping I wasn't rushing to a crime scene. I'd thought about alerting the Lewisburg city police, but ex-cons aren't overly fond of police officers showing up at their doors, and there was the possibility that he'd panic. I decided it was better going it alone, at least for now.

I'd responded to suicide calls before, but they were all from the hospital ER, failed attempts by people who'd overdosed on pills. Women usually chose this method, which meant they were more likely to survive suicide attempts than men were. This was the first time I was confronting someone who was actively suicidal. I kept reminding myself that he'd gone to the trouble to call me, which suggested he really didn't want to harm himself. I screeched to a stop in front of his apartment building, took the stairs two at a time and knocked on the door.

"Come on in," he said. And there he was, the captain of the tennis team, all blond hair and white teeth, sitting at his kitchen table with a knife that looked like it could skin a wild boar.

"Good to see you, Brody," I said calmly. His legs were in constant motion and he looked wired, like he was on something stronger than coffee. In the 70's amphetamines were the recreational drugs of choice. Druggies had grown tired of LSD, and cocaine, crack, and meth labs hadn't come into fashion yet. Brody had been a speed freak before he'd gone to prison, but he was supposed to be clean now.

"I hate this, man," he said, without being specific.

"What do you hate?"

"This fuckin' dump," he gestured at the walls with his knife. "I liked it better at the Fellowship Home. Hell, the state pen was better than this shit-hole."

I saw what he meant. Some of the downtown apartments were little more than afterthoughts, what business owners did with upstairs spaces to try to squeeze more income out of their properties. There were a few airy lofts with high ceilings and tall windows, but they were pricey and they stayed occupied. The low rent units were claustrophobic little affairs with sunless windows. "Was this the best your parole officer could come up with?"

"I guess. She told me she found a really cheap place that was already furnished."

"I'll bet living here by yourself really gets on your nerves." He'd already told me so, but I was shifting to the active listening mode to keep him talking. "You like having people around, don't you?"

"Yeah, man, I like hangin' out. If I meet a chick I can't bring her up here. Only skanks would come in this place."

"You look like you can do better than skanks."

"I can get girls," he said confidently.

"Isn't sex a good enough reason to keep on living?"

He shrugged.

"Brody, are you serious about killing yourself or do you just want company?"

"You think I'm kiddin'?" He picked up the knife and stabbed it in the table forcefully. The sharp point cut through the wood like it was a stick of butter.

"Are you back on drugs?"

"No."

I had a feeling he was lying. I also thought he wasn't depressed or suicidal. It's hard to be wired and depressed at the same time. Speed freaks are prone to having suicidal thoughts when they're coming down from benders, but he wasn't coming down. "Brody, I don't think you're being honest with me," I challenged him. "I think you're still on speed. I'll make you an offer. Tomorrow I'll call your probation officer and tell her this isn't a good setup for you. We'll let you move back into the Fellowship Home until she can find you a better place. But you can't live at the Fellowship Home and use drugs."

"What if I do?"

"We'll have to kick you out. If that happens the court might revoke your parole and send you back to Huttonsville."

"If I go back to the Fellowship Home will you guys help me get a job?"

"We can try." I didn't want to promise anything. Most of our local employers weren't interested hiring a paroled drug dealer. The few who might give it a shot had jobs to offer like cleaning out septic tanks or stunning cattle in slaughterhouses. I couldn't see Brody pursuing either of these lines of work.

"You really gonna get me out of this place?"

"Are you really going to stay clean?"

"Yeah, I promise." A druggie's promise isn't worth much. People who are strongly attracted to alcohol or drugs are usually trying to medicate themselves. Hyperactive people liked downers. Slackers liked uppers. People who were generally unhappy with their lives liked hallucinogens. Few had any insight into their behavior, just an inclination to take the easiest road. Brody probably wasn't going to quit cold turkey just because he had prison hanging over his head. But I had to give him a chance anyway.

"Okay, I'll talk to your parole officer and I'll talk to Hank about letting you go back to the Fellowship Home."

"You're a helluva guy," he said. "How many people would come out in the middle of the night to talk some asshole with a knife?"

"This is my job and I get paid for it. And you're not an asshole, Brody. I'll make you another offer."

"What?"

"I'm teaching a class at Concord College. I'd like you to come to one of my classes and tell them about your time in prison. I think you'd make a strong impression. I'm sure at least a couple of my students use speed to stay awake or study or whatever. When they hear how it snowballed in your case, they might have second thoughts."

"You want *me* to talk to a college class?"

"Sure. I'm bringing in guest speakers who know about different aspects of the correctional system. You have a different kind of expertise than anybody else. I think they need to hear from you."

"I've never been to a college before."

"I think you'll like it. You don't have to give a speech. All you've got to do is tell them your story and answer their questions."

"What if I say the wrong thing?"

"No such thing. Your story is your story. Your feelings are your feelings. It's a night class. I'll buy you a steak when we get done."

"Are there any good-looking chicks at this college?"

"Tons."

He smiled. Even if he wasn't suicidal I'd given him something to live for.

I took the knife with me, but it was just a gesture. I wanted him to feel like we cared.

By now it was eleven-thirty. As I drove south on Church Street, past the mental health clinic, I noticed a light in the front office. I slowed down and I saw a strange woman pawing through our file cabinets. This wasn't good. I parked up the street, walked back stealthily and watched her through the window. She was rummaging through the files. She found the one she wanted, sat down at the desk and opened it. Needless to say mental health records are highly confidential, so this was serious business. Since it involved a break-in, I decided to find the police instead of charging in and confronting her myself.

When I left Brody's apartment I saw a cruiser idling in front of city hall, so I found the officer and told him what I'd witnessed. When we arrived at the clinic the woman was still sitting at the desk, reading the file with obvious interest. "She's pretty brazen," the policeman observed. "You'd think she'd at least use a flashlight." The front door was locked. This meant she'd broken in through this door and locked it behind her, or she'd gained access through the fire exit or a window. I slid my key quietly in the lock and turned it. The officer nodded. "Let's go."

We rushed into the office and startled her. "I'll take that," I snatched the file from her. I glanced at the name: Jennifer Albright, one of Anne Blair's clients.

"Ma'am," the officer addressed her more politely than the situation called for, "would you mind explaining what you're doing in the Greenbrier Valley Mental Health Clinic in the middle of the night, reading a confidential file?"

"I work here," she insisted.

He looked at me questioningly.

"I've been here six months and I've never seen her." She was fiftyish. She had brown hair with blonde highlights, and she was wearing stylish glasses. She looked more put-together than the kind of person you'd expect to catch committing a nighttime burglary.

She looked at me. "Who are you?"

"Greg Johnson. I'm the clinic's social worker. I happened to be driving by and I saw you going through our file cabinets."

"What's your name, ma'am?" the officer asked her.

"Margo Hodges."

I gasped. "Oh my God, you're Margo!"

"I'm a licensed clinical psychologist," she explained to the policeman. "And I'm the clinical director."

The police officer looked at me questioningly. "Is this true?"

"Yes," I admitted.

"She works here and you've never met her?"

It was too hard to explain, so I didn't bother trying. "She's legitimate. Margo's been on the staff for years."

"Twelve," she said to the officer. "Anne Blair asked me to do a psychological evaluation on one of her clients. I was just going over her background. Everyone knows I'm a night person."

I handed the file back to her sheepishly. "Sorry."

"So everything's okay?" the policeman double-checked.

"Everything's fine. Thanks for your help."

"You look tired, Johnson," he said. "Go home and go to bed."

"Gladly." I turned to Margo. "Will you be around tomorrow?"

"Yes."

"Maybe we can get to know each other better." It was like discovering there really was a Santa Claus. "Oh, and thanks for all the postcards."

She looked pleased. "You're welcome. I didn't know if anybody read them."

"Oh we read them," I guaranteed her. "Every week."

Chapter 15
One Toque Over the Line

One of the things I liked about working at the clinic was learning about other people's lives. If a client mentioned that she used to live in Newfoundland, curiosity would get the better of me and I'd pepper her with questions. I didn't need all this background information, but it made the job more interesting.

Someone who really pulled back the curtain gave me a behind-the-scenes glimpse at her life was Maggie Hayes, a culinary apprentice at The Greenbrier. Maggie claimed she was 29, but she looked like 29-and-holding. She was a tough little fireplug of a woman; I could imagine her smoking a stogie. She showed up for her appointment in her chef's whites. "Sorry I'm dressed like this," she apologized in her husky voice. "I'm pulling a split shift. I pulled five-to-ten this morning and I'm pulling two-to ten-this evening."

"You don't get much sleep, do you?"

"I grabbed some z's in a linen closet yesterday," came her surprising answer. "We live in staff housing behind the hotel. When I'm pulling a split shift I don't feel like walking over there and coming back. I know a closet no one uses, so I crash in it."

"If you're that creative, you must be a good cook."

"Yeah, tell that to my supervisor."

"Problems?"

"Buddy, I've got problems up the wazoo. I've got so many I don't even know where to start."

"Why don't you tell me about the apprentice program," I suggested. "It might help me understand what you're going through."

"I'm going through hell. Last month I filed a complaint about my supervisor with the union. He's getting even with me. I should be working in the main kitchen, but he's got me flipping burgers and warming up leftovers in the Chatterbox."

"The Chatterbox?"

"The employee cafeteria."

"What brought you to the culinary program, Maggie?"

"I was an Air Force brat. When I was in high school we were stationed at MacDill Air Force Base in Tampa and I got a job at Steak 'n Shake. The girls waited tables and the guys ran the grill. I hated dealing with the customers so they let me cook. I've been doing restaurant work ever since. Every time some asshole manager gave me a hard time, I'd quit and get a better job. People told me I should go to CIA."

"What's CIA?"

"This hoity-toity place in New York, the Culinary Institute of America. It costs an arm and a leg and I couldn't afford it. A friend told me about The Greenbrier's apprentice program. It's a two-year deal, and they pay you instead of you paying them. They take eight or ten apprentices a year. They weren't so sure about me. They let me work at the hotel for a year to see if I was cut out for it. Guess they thought I was – they let me in."

"Do you take classes?"

"Nah, you follow the chefs around and do whatever they tell you. My first day one of them yelled at me, 'Make me a Mornay sauce!' I ran over to someone and I asked him, 'What the hell's a Mornay sauce?' He said, 'It's a béchamel sauce with cheese.' I said, 'Great, I'll get right on it.' "

"So it's all learning by doing?"

"It's learning by working your patootie off. You sweat over a stove for hours and sling 50-pound kettles around."

"How far along are you?"

"I'm a senior. I shouldn't be in the Chatterbox! I shouldn't be pulling split shifts! I shouldn't be slicing and dicing! You do that stuff when you start out. He's got it in for me."

"What should you be doing?"

"Pulling straight shifts in the main kitchen. Meats and sauces. If I'm on the veg station, I should be running it, not working the line."

"Do you do any baking?"

"That's another department, down in the basement. When you start out you've got to decide if you want to cook or bake. You're either upstairs or you're downstairs. If you ask me, baking's boring. There's a reason grandma's sugar cookies always taste the same. She puts the exact same ingredients in 'em the exact same way. If you asked her to throw in some pineapple or toasted coconut, she'd go ape shit."

I tried to picture my grandmother going ape shit. It was a stretch.

"Baking's a science," she continued my culinary education. "Cooking's an art. You season something until it tastes right. You play around with presentation. You come up with new dishes. Famous chefs make tons of money. Famous bakers? Hah! Name one."

I took the bait. "Betty Crocker?"

"She never existed. They made her up to sell cake mixes."

"Sara Lee?"

"Some guy named his company after his daughter."

"Duncan Hines?"

"Duncan Hines was a food critic. He wrote restaurant guidebooks."

I noticed she was perched on the edge of her chair. "Is that chair uncomfortable? I can get you another one."

"Nah, I'm just not used to sitting down. That's why I like kitchen work. You're always doing something. We're doing ice sculptures in a couple of months and I've been practicing with a chain saw. Some of the guys think women can't handle chain saws. I'm gonna show 'em."

"Are most of the chefs men?"

"There aren't many women. There's this incredible lady from Thailand, but she doesn't get much credit because she's just a little Asian lady. If she was a man from Germany and she cooked the same way, they'd think she was a genius. There's a pecking order. The Europeans are on top. Don't get me wrong, they're great chefs.

They started back in the Old Country when they were twelve or thirteen."

"How's the pay?"

"We make about half what the regular staff do, but we get tons of overtime."

"What was your complaint to the union?"

"My supervisor was hitting on me. He was bumping up against me and giving me these looks."

"What kind of looks?"

"The kind you'd have to be a woman to understand."

Maggie wasn't exactly a femme fatale. She seemed an unlikely target for sexual advances, but you never knew. In the 70's the good old boy system was still firmly in place, and her bosses and union officials probably would have taken her complaint with a grain of salt. Her supervisor would have suffered a token reprimand at best, and some wisecracks from his friends.

"What do you hope to accomplish by coming to the clinic?" I asked her. "How can we help you?"

"I'm stressed out. You guys help people handle stress, don't you?"

"Sure. We can even give you a medical excuse to take a few days off."

"I don't want any days off. I'd just have to come back to the same old crap."

"Do you want to quit the program?"

"Hell, no! I want to graduate! I've put too much into all this."

"We have a therapist named Penelope who teaches stress reduction," I told her. "I can give you an appointment to see her."

"Okay."

"But that's not going to fix the situation with your supervisor, Maggie. If you think he's the kind of man who'll only listen to another man, I'll be glad to have a little chat with him."

She wasn't expecting this offer, and it seemed to intrigue her. She inched forward in her chair. "What would you say?"

"I'd say there seems to be some kind of misunderstanding between the two of you and it's stressing you out so much that you came to the clinic for help. I'd tell him you want to finish the program, and I'd ask him to help you work things out. I won't accuse him of anything. I'll listen to what he has to say and encourage him to patch things up with you."

"What if he gets pissed?"

"If I get chased out of The Greenbrier by a chef with a cleaver, I'll have a great story to tell my grandkids."

"If he chops off your balls you won't have any grandkids."

Maggie minced garlic and onions, not words.

Chef Jean-Claude Legrande was surprised when I called and asked to meet with him, but he agreed to give me a few minutes of his valuable time. I knew it was valuable because he pointed this out twice in our short conversation.

When I went looking for him at the hotel, the first thing I noticed was that The Greenbrier's celebrated romance-and-rhododendrons theme stopped at the kitchen doors. I had suddenly gone from pink flowers and bold stripes into an industrial workspace. A large electronic scoreboard hung from the ceiling. I was puzzled by this sporting arena touch until I saw they were using it to keep track of the orders coming into the kitchen. When you're serving a thousand people, it helps to know how many Carpaccio of Beef Tenderloins you need to plate.

The kitchen was alive with activity, and the workers barely noticed me. Off to one side a long table was set for fine dining with linen, china and stemware. This was the chefs' table, but not the kind of VIP tasting table that would become popular in restaurant kitchens in later years. This was where The Greenbrier's top chefs were served their own meals by the staff. The message was clear: a kitchen isn't a democracy. I approached the chef's table with trepidation, wondering what I was getting myself into.

"Hi," I greeted them with a smile. "I'm looking for Chef Legrande."

A flock of white toques turned in my direction and gave me the kind of looks you'd get from the College of Cardinals if you'd interrupted them while they were electing the next pope. A man near the head of the table spoke up. "I am Jean-Claude Legrande," he said in the suave-but-snooty manner Frenchmen love to cultivate.

"Hi, Chef," I braved on. "I'm Greg Johnson. I called about meeting with you this afternoon?"

"What are you doing in zee kitchen?"

"You told me I could find you here."

"Wait for me out zere!" He pointed at the doors, gave a loud snort and returned to his plate of scallops.

Minutes crawled by as I idled in the hallway. I was about to give up and leave when the doors flew open.

"What do you want?" he asked me.

"I work at the mental health clinic in Lewisburg," I refreshed his memory. "Maggie Hayes came to the clinic because she's having some work-related stress and she's afraid she might not make it through your culinary program. Is there someplace we can talk privately?"

He turned on his heels and marched me to a nearby office. He didn't offer me a seat, so I knew he wanted to keep this brief. "Elle est folle," he informed me, pointing at his head and twirling his finger. I didn't know French, but I got the message. "She thinks I desi-rez her! She thinks I desi-rez une affaire. How can I desi-rez her? She is not Brigitte Bardot! She is not Catherine Deneuve! She is not Sophia Loren! Elle est folle!"

"I don't know Maggie very well," I admitted. "How's she doing in your program?"

"She is good wiz zee culinaire. I cannot fire her because it would look like I am trying to hide une affaire. Zere is no affaire! If I desi-rez one, I find for me someone better zan her."

"Is this a recent development or has it been going on for awhile?"

He held up a finger. "One month. Before that she thinks I am fantastique."

"What do you suppose gave her the idea that you're interested in her?"

He leaned forward. His toque towered over me. "You want to know what I think?"

"Yes, that's why I'm here."

"She desi-rez Jean-Claude Legrande! She is upset because I do not desi-rez her! She thinks all Frenchmen desi-rez affaires."

"Don't they?" I teased him.

"With her? Nev-aire!" He made a face like he'd bitten into a lemon.

I left with the knowledge that the chef was assigning Maggie to the Chatterbox to avoid any more of what he considered false accusations. This was having the unfortunate side effect of keeping her from the culinary epicenter exactly when she needed to be in it.

Like a hollandaise, the plot was thickening.

When Maggie visited the clinic again I pressed her for more details. "Tell me about the sexual harassment, Maggie. What exactly did Chef Legrande do?"

"He rubbed up against me and made disgusting noises."

"What kind of noises?"

"Grunting noises."

"He kind of makes those anyway, doesn't he?" She didn't say anything. "Were you working in close quarters? Any chance he might have bumped against you by accident?"

"Not if you saw the way he looked."

"Did he proposition you?"

"Not in so many words, but I knew what he wanted."

"How did you know?"

"Women have a radar for that kind of stuff."

I tried to gather facts, but it seemed there were few to gather. The Chef's fervent denials had created doubts in my mind, and Maggie wasn't doing anything to dispel them. "I'll be honest with you, Maggie," I leveled with her. "If I were a lawyer and you came to me with this story, I'd say you had a weak case. You need more evidence."

She sprang from her chair. "You're just like that damn union rep!"

"Chef Legrande seems as upset about this as you are. He's assigning you to the Chatterbox because he's afraid to have you in the same place where he's working. I don't see how you can resolve this unless you're both willing to write it off to some kind of misunderstanding and give each other another chance."

"You men always stick together," she said angrily. "I should have asked for a woman counselor."

"I can set you up to see Penelope. I'm sure you'd like her."

"I don't want your damn help!" She got up and bolted for the door.

"Maggie, please wait."

She looked back. "For what? The first time I talked to you I thought you were so great. But if you're what these mental health places are all about, it's just a big waste of time." She slammed the door and I heard her angry clops echoing in the stairwell.

I went to see our psychiatrist Pete. He loved human puzzles, and he always had an opinion. "Sounds like borderline personality disorder," he diagnosed. He ticked off the clues. "She put you on a pedestal and shoved you off. She did the same thing with the chef. She's had a lot of jobs, which suggests a pattern of instability. She's hyperactive. She overreacts. She seems a little paranoid. When someone presents with a whole grab bag of symptoms like these, borderline's the first thing you need to rule out. If it's true, it's going to take more than two or three sessions to straighten her out. She needs long-term treatment."

"Are you saying she would have acted like this no matter what I did?"

"Probably. You want to deal with happy, well-adjusted folks? Get a job somewhere else."

"Thanks for putting it in perspective."

"I could be wrong," he said. "But take a look at the diagnostic criteria in the DSM. I think you'll recognize her."

The next day I was heading to lunch when Jayne called me into the front office. "I've got something for you," she said. She gave me a Tupperware container. "Maggie Hayes came by and left this for you. She asked to see you, but you were with a client."

I read the handwritten label. "Pumpkin Lobster Bisque?" I cracked the lid and a heavenly aroma filled the office.

"Wow," Jayne reacted.

I hurried to Pete's office with the soup and interrupted him while he was writing case notes. "Remember the chef from the hotel I told you about yesterday? I think I misjudged her. Look what she brought me." I put the container on his desk and opened the lid. "I'll share it with you."

He eyed the soup warily. "I'd be careful with that. You might be dealing with a sick puppy. She could be trying to poison you."

"You're kidding, aren't you?"

"I'm serious as hell. I wouldn't touch the stuff."

I took a whiff. "Smells pretty damned good for poison."

"She's a professional chef," he said. "Who would know better how to mask the smell of poison? I hope you're not actually thinking about eating it."

"Yes, I am. I'll let you know if it kills me."

"Let me see that," he said. I handed him the container. I thought he was going to give it a closer inspection, but before I knew what was happening he was in his bathroom, pouring the soup down the toilet.

I ran in. "Pete! What are you doing?"

"Sparing you the agony," he said as he flushed my bisque into Lewisburg's sewer system.

"Pete, that was *my* soup! A chef from a five star resort made that for me!"

"Better safe than sorry. You can't be too careful in this business."

"I don't believe you did that!"

Anne Blair's office was next to Pete's. She heard us arguing and she poked her head in the door. "What's going on with you two?"

"Pete flushed my soup down the toilet!"

He eyed me with amusement. "You sound like a kindergartener tattling on the class bully."

"What am I supposed to tell my client when she asks how I liked her pumpkin lobster bisque?"

"Tell her you loved it."

I tried to reach Maggie at the hotel, but she'd given us the number of a pay phone in the staff quarters. On the rare occasion someone answered it, they told me she was at work. Since I hadn't heard from her, I figured she'd managed to smooth things out with Jean-Claude. I needed more closure, so I gave him a call.

"Maggie left the culinaire program," he gave me the news.

"That's too bad," I reacted.

"She is cra-zee, but she will always find work. She is not cut out for Zee Green-briere, but she is still very good."

"I'm sure she'd appreciate hearing you say that."

"Her soups," he added almost wistfully, "were magnifique."

Chapter 16
A Tale of Two Lectures

In a lifetime of impulsive behavior, the impulse that worked out best for me wasn't moving to West Virginia or going into social work or looking for a job in the Greenbrier Valley. It was inviting Libby Meadows to a get-acquainted pizza party for the social work students at Concord College.

Libby was beautiful, warm and intelligent. No matter how attractive or smart a person is, if they lack warmth, something big is missing. All the Dale Carnegie courses in the world can't teach you how to be warm. People who genuinely care about other people seem to have been born that way, and people who are cold and impersonal seem to have always been that way, too. Libby was radiant, outgoing and down-to-earth. I knew right away I didn't have to try to impress her. It's a relief to know that you don't have to impress someone; it saves an awful lot of trouble. She was curious about my job, and I was curious about the fact that she'd spent the last year apprenticing with a potter, despite the fact that she had a degree from West Virginia Wesleyan College. She'd lived in New Mexico for two summers and she knew a lot about Native Americans and their handcrafts. But even with this interest she was thinking about teaching school because it was a more stable life.

When I went by her parents' home to pick her up, her father was planting some forsythia bushes in the backyard. "The first year they sleep, the second year they creep and the third year they leap," he shared a little landscaping wisdom. When we got to Concord and met the students, I realized this was a pretty good description of college life, too. Freshmen are easily distracted. Sophomores are starting to pay more attention, especially if they're coming off academic probation. Juniors and seniors are more serious about the whole thing because they're closer to having to go out in the real world and support themselves. I was pleased to discover that my corrections class was made up mostly of juniors and seniors. They seemed ready to leap. Concord's students hailed mostly from the southern part of the state, including the coalfields in the southwest. They were young people from blue-collar families, transitioning to white-collar jobs. There's a certain basic humility and decency in West Virginians, and I saw it in the students I met at the party. I liked them and I liked the other faculty. I really liked Libby. Instead of spending the evening hanging around with me she circulated and met the students. It seemed like the right thing to do, and I was impressed.

Once our class got rolling I realized I knew a little more about the subject matter than I'd thought. After five or six months at the clinic I'd had plenty of exposure to lawyers and court proceedings. Still, I lacked the expertise you'd hope a professor would have. Giving these students a real education hinged on finding the right guest speakers. I jumped right in, bringing in a juvenile probation officer, a parole officer and a prosecuting attorney. Word got around that the course was interesting and I had a brief flurry of students wanting to add it. We ended up with twenty in the class.

The fourth week I hit a home run with Circuit Court Judge Charles M. Lobban. Charlie was one of the first people I'd met in Greenbrier County. He sometimes ate lunch with Anne Blair and her cronies at the Court Restaurant, and she'd introduced us on my first day of work. He was pleased to learn that I was living in Alderson, his hometown. The judge was jovial and expansive. He was a longtime member of the Alderson Volunteer Fire Department and he suggested that I join it. His sons Charlie and John were firefighters, and so was his nephew H.R. His brother-in-law Howard was the fire chief. When

I asked Charlie to speak to my class he readily agreed, even though it meant a two-hour round trip and giving up an evening at home.

As we drove to the campus he told me the story of his unlikely path to the bench. His late father, Floyd G. Lobban, had owned a furniture store in Alderson. When Charlie finished law school he didn't see any reason to rent an office since his father owned a building, so he opened a law office in the back of the store. His clients would make their ways past sofas and bedroom suites, and he would draw up their wills and handle their real estate transactions and criminal matters. On slow days he made furniture deliveries. This would seem like a waste of a lawyer's time, but judges are elected in West Virginia and his deliveries paid off when he ran for office. He'd visited so many homes that the voters felt like they knew him personally. He won in a landslide. People talked about how likeable he was and how well he treated everyone in his courtroom; some defendants actually thanked him after he sentenced them to prison.

From the moment he started speaking he had the students' full attention. "There are two kinds of judges," he told them. "The kind who know the law and the kind who think they are the law. If you ever go to court, you want the first kind. But there are plenty of the second kind still around." His observation rang true.

He posed an interesting question to the students. "Who's the most powerful person in our judicial system?" Most of them said it was the judge. Someone who thought she was being clever said the juror. "The single most powerful person in our judicial system is the prosecuting attorney," he told them. "The prosecutor decides whether to bring a case to trial. Let's say Jimmy and his friend are out drinking and on the way home he runs off the road and his friend is thrown from the car and dies. I don't decide if Jimmy should be charged with negligent homicide, the prosecutor does. Our prosecutor in Greenbrier County is Ralph Hayes. In a situation like this Ralph would take a lot of things into account, including how the family of the deceased feels about it. If they come to him and say, "We don't see what good it's going to do to prosecute Jimmy. Our son is gone and we'll never be able to do anything about it. He wouldn't want to see his best friend prosecuted for this." With that kind of merciful sentiment, Ralph might decide not to prosecute, especially if Jimmy's in the hospital with serious injuries himself. I don't bring cases to trial. I just schedule them. I don't determine a defendant's guilt or innocence; the jury does. Just because I'm sitting up there in a fancy robe looking down on everyone doesn't mean I control the whole process."

A student named Wally raised his hand. "Then what does a judge do?"

"A judge is an umpire," he put it in language they could understand. "A judge sees that the rules of the court are followed like an umpire sees that the rules of baseball are followed. In addition, if a defendant is found guilty or accepts a plea agreement, the judge does the sentencing. Sentencing sounds like the easy part, doesn't it?"

Heads bobbed. "Okay, I'll tell you a story. You be the judge. You tell me how you would sentence this person."

He described an upstanding member of the community, a model husband and father, a deacon in the Baptist Church, a member of the Rotary Club, who had been keeping the books for a local company. Over a five-year period he had embezzled $180,000 dollars from the company. "Would you give him probation or sentence him to prison?" he asked them.

After some discussion the students agreed they would ignore the defendant's standing in the community and send him to prison. One student captured the general consensus when he said, "Just because he's a deacon and a member of the Rotary Club doesn't mean he should be treated special. He still stole the money."

"Okay," the judge said. "So let's sentence him to one-to-ten and move on to the next case. This case is the same situation but it involves the man's father, who owned the bookkeeping company with him and embezzled the same money. The father is 68 years old, has congestive heart failure and a wife dying of cancer. He drives her to Roanoke three times a week for her cancer treatments. How would you sentence him?"

The students debated it for a while and they ended up recommending probation.

"But what about equal treatment?" Judge Lobban asked them. "Why shouldn't two people who committed the same crime get the same punishment?"

"The situations are different," someone pointed out. "If you send the father off to prison, he'll probably die there while his wife dies of cancer."

"That's why sentencing isn't as easy as it sounds," the judge said. It was a simple but clever illustration. Charlie knew that social work students wouldn't want to see a thief get preferential treatment because of his high status in the community. But he also knew they wouldn't want to incarcerate a sickly man with a dying wife. "Now remember," he added, "the man you're sending to prison will probably be there when his parents die. If he stayed at home he could help them. Do you still want to lock him up?" The students squirmed. In the end they decided to give both men probation on the grounds that their crimes weren't violent, neither presented a threat to society, and they would be more likely to be able to make restitution for the crime if they had employment.

He gave them some other cases. By the end of the class they wanted to become judges instead of social workers.

"How do you get to be a judge?" someone asked him.

Charlie chuckled and looked at me. "Deliver a lot of furniture."

Charlie knew I was dating Libby. He and his wife Marjorie were close friends with her parents, Joe and Ruth. On the way back to Alderson he gave me his two cents. "She's a lovely girl from a wonderful family," he said. "People don't get any finer than Joe and Ruth Meadows."

"Libby's perfect," I said.

He smiled. "You've got it pretty bad, don't you?"

"Yeah, I do," I admitted.

Two weeks later I brought in a speaker who was the judge's polar opposite. Brody, my paroled drug dealer, was making his first visit to a college campus. He hadn't been in a place with so many young women since he was in high school, and his eyes were bugging out as we made our way from the parking lot to the building. "If the guys at The Hut could see me now, they'd shit," he said. When we walked into the classroom, the young women sat up and took notice. It was one thing to bring a middle-aged judge or probation officer to class, but another to bring a good-looking guy closer to their age.

"Our guest speaker tonight has a very different story to tell than the other people who've been here," I said by way of introduction. "Brody Allen is from Greenbrier County. For the past two years he's been an inmate at Huttonsville Correctional Center. Huttonsville is a medium-security prison in a rural area of Randolph County. When it opened in the 1930's the idea was to have the inmates do farm work and grow their own food. They still raise beef, but they've added other kinds of job training since most of the inmates aren't going to be farming when they go home. I told Brody he didn't have to give a lecture – just tell you about his experiences and answer your questions. So I'll turn things over to him and he can give us an insider's look at our state correctional system."

Brody took a seat on the desk and threw one leg over the corner in a devil-may-care manner. "So what do you guys want to know?"

"What were you in for?" someone got the ball rolling.

"Dealin' speed. You guys know what that is?"

"Amphetamines," a student named Joe said.

"Yep. I was makin' good money 'til a narc set me up and four pigs busted me. They charged me with intent to deliver. My lawyer told me I could get one-to-five and have to pay fifteen grand. He had me plead guilty to a lesser charge."

I cut in, "Remember what Judge Lobban said about the prosecutor being the most powerful person in the judicial system? Plea bargains are a good example. The prosecuting attorney has to agree to let a defendant plead to a lesser charge. Why would a prosecutor be willing to offer that kind of deal to someone?"

"To avoid a trial?" a student named Karen guessed.

"Yes. But why not have a trial? Isn't that what courts do?"

"They cost money and take time," she said. "They can't afford to give everyone a trial."

"Exactly."

Wally spoke up again. "Or maybe the evidence isn't so strong. Maybe the prosecutor would rather have the defendant plead guilty to a lesser crime than risk losing the case."

"You're right. The reasons Karen and Wally have given explain why 95% of all felony cases are settled through plea bargains. Our judicial system would collapse if all these cases went to trial. You might think the world has too many lawyers, but there aren't nearly enough to handle the thousands of trials that would result if we didn't have plea agreements. On TV everyone has a trial, but it doesn't work that way in reality."

"But doesn't a plea bargain assume a person is guilty?" a student named Chris asked. "They must be offering plea bargains to innocent people, too."

"Good point," I agreed. "Some innocent people end up accepting plea agreements because they're afraid they'll be found guilty of a worse crime and get a harsher sentence. They give up their constitutional rights out of fear."

"It doesn't seem right," Chris responded.

"The whole system's set up to screw you," Brody stepped in. "My lawyer could'a cared less if they shipped my ass off to prison for the rest of my life. He wasn't worth shit."

"Did you hire your own lawyer?" someone asked him.

"Nah, they gave me one. That's another way they screw you."

The students were taking all this in. I hoped they noticed the discrepancy between his claim that he'd made a lot of money as a dealer and his inability to afford a lawyer.

"Any of you guys ever been to a prison?" he asked them.

No one had. He told them about life at Huttonsville. The students were surprised to learn that the inmates lived in a military-style barracks instead of in cells, which was common in medium-security facilities and prison camps. He explained that he'd been able to leave the grounds with a crew that did roadwork and state park maintenance. "But I hated wearin' an orange jumpsuit," he said.

"Orange isn't your color?" one of the girls asked him.

"People drive by and look at you like you're a rapist or a murders or somethin'," he replied.

He told them that the prison officials had encouraged him to participate in drug counseling. "I did it so they wouldn't make me have to do it when I got out,' he explained his motive. "I knew more than the damn counselor. I didn't learn nothin'."

A student named Angela raised her hand. "Brody, do you feel anything positive happened to you in prison?"

"Gettin' my G.E.D.," he said.

I had a question of my own. "Would you say Huttonsville focuses more on punishment or rehabilitation?"

"Punishment," he said, which didn't fit the institution he'd just described.

"Did you learn any lessons?" Chris asked him.

"I learned plenty," he said with a smirk. "I learned how to get in touch with every dealer in West Virginia."

Joe put him on the spot. "You think you'll go back to selling drugs?"

He shrugged. Even if he was planning to give it up, he was too cool to admit it.

"What did you think of Brody?" I asked the students in our follow-up session on Thursday.

"I think he's already on his way back to prison," Karen predicted. "He wants to blame everyone but himself. He blames the police, he blames his lawyer, he blames the court, he blames the drug counselors. He thinks he's smarter than everyone else."

"Did you guys get the idea that he was trying to show off?" Wally asked his classmates. There was a general consensus that he was.

"You've got to cut the guy some slack," Chris opined. "He just got out of prison. He was probably nervous being here. He probably thought he needed to act like a big man to impress us."

"Yeah right, Chris," Wally had a less generous opinion. "Underneath it all Brody's a real sensitive guy."

"Did you see anything positive about him?" I asked them.

"He's good-looking," Angela said. Everyone laughed.

"Angie's going to marry a sociopath," Joe teased her.

"I didn't say I want to marry him!"

"Joe," I followed up on his comment, "you just used the word sociopath. Can you tell us what a sociopath is?"

"You should tell us," he tried to turn the tables. "You work in mental health."

"Just give it a shot."

He thought about it for a minute. "A sociopath is someone who's self-centered and doesn't care about other people. He's totally irresponsible. He lies and he steals and he mistreats the people that are trying to be good to him. He can't form relationships. He thinks the normal rules don't apply to him."

"That's very good, Joe. See me after class."

"What'd I say?" he asked. "Am I in trouble?"

"No. Just see me after class."

The students had picked up on the things I'd hoped. We spent the rest of the session talking about punishment versus rehabilitation, and whether anyone could be rehabilitated. They decided it came down to personality and attitude; some people could and some people couldn't. My favorite comment came from Karen.

"You can see why Judge Lobban ended up where he did and why Brody's ended up where he has," she observed.

Joe waited after class. When the others were gone I made him an offer he wasn't expecting. "I was impressed with your description of sociopaths," I told him. "Would you be interested in doing your internship at the Greenbrier Valley Mental Health Clinic?"

He smiled. "Yeah."

"We pay our interns, by the way."

"Then hell yes," he said with an even bigger smile.

"I'll talk to Buford about it. You'll be counseling Brody, by the way."

His smile faded and he looked worried. "Really?"

"No, I'm just giving you a hard time. The worst news is that I'll be your supervisor."

"I can handle that," he said. He left the classroom feeling ten feet tall.

Chapter 17
Better Safe

I shared several clients with Jack McManus, who worked at the Lewisburg office of the state's Vocational Rehabilitation division. They were people with developmental disabilities or psychological issues who needed job training. In addition to plugging people in with employers who could teach them job skills, Jack's agency also ran a training facility west of Charleston in a community called Institute. The unincorporated town's name dates back to when it was the home of the West Virginia Colored Institute, which later became West Virginia State University.

The local Rehab office was a block from the mental health clinic. Whenever Jack wanted something he usually came by in person, but today he called to give me some bad news. "I'm in the hospital," he said. "I had a heart attack. I'm going to be off work for a while."

"Wow. How could you have a heart attack? You're only in your forties, Jack. You look like you're in pretty good shape."

"I should have picked my ancestors more carefully."

"How are you doing?"

"I'm still on top of the grass."

"That's comforting."

We talked about his health, but the conversation soon moved on to another reason he was calling. "Do you remember Medwin Bales?"

"The guy who was born on a roller coaster?"

"The one and only. He was supposed to go to Institute in August for janitorial training, but when he went to work at the State Fair he lost his slot in the program. They've got another opening now and they're holding it for him. I'm supposed to take him this week, but obviously that's not going to happen. He doesn't know the other counselors in our office. He thinks you're his buddy because you got him the job at the donut stand. Would you mind driving him to Institute and getting him squared away?"

"That's the least I can do for you. Are you sure Medwin's going to cooperate this time?"

"Unless his mother sabotages it. She's a little odd herself."

"I hear she had her second child on a seesaw."

"Don't make me laugh. It hurts enough already."

The Bales family lived in an unpainted cabin that faced a creek. A footbridge led over the creek to the house. It was a beautiful setting, the kind of place that would have made a good hunting or fishing camp. When I parked in front I saw Medwin in the creek, filling some plastic bottles with water. Mrs. Bales was in the yard with a can of paint, putting the finishing touches on a sign that read "No Tress Passing With Out Permission".

"May I have permission to trespass?" I requested.

"Yeah, come on," she invited me.

Halfway across the bridge I stopped and looked down at Medwin. "Are you planning to drink that water?"

"Yeah."

"Are you going to purify it first?"

"Water's pure after it passes over seven rocks," his mother informed me.

"Really?"

"I thought everybody knew that," she said.

Apparently this purification system hadn't killed anyone in the family yet. I turned back to Medwin. "Are you ready to go to Institute?"

"He's not going," his mother said. "Medwin doesn't need to be in an institution."

"It's not an institution, Mrs. Bales, it's a training center. It's in a town called Institute. The name's confusing, but it's like a school. He's not going to be locked up. They'll help him learn a skill so he can get a job and support himself."

She gave me a doubtful look. "If it's not an institution why do they call it one?"

"It's in a town called Institute," I repeated.

"That's the damnedest thing I've ever heard."

"It's a good program. They'll help him find a job after he finishes."

"How long would he be there?"

"Probably about six months. It depends on how fast he learns a skill."

"Medwin's a fast learner. He takes after me."

"That's great."

While Medwin packed, Mrs. Bales educated me on subjects great and small. I admired her pumpkin patch and she warned me never to swallow pumpkin or watermelon seeds because they can grow in your stomach. She told me that the New River was the only river in the world that flowed north. I was tempted to point out that the nearby Shenandoah also flowed north, up through the Shenandoah Valley and into the Potomac at Harper's Ferry, but what really mattered was Medwin's direction, not the river's, so I held my tongue. Eventually we made our escape.

When we arrived at the Rehab Center he was surprised to see mobility impaired clients in wheelchairs, and blind people tapping along the sidewalk with canes. I explained to him that some of the center's clients had physical disabilities. "I can push the people in the wheelchairs," he said, and I knew he was going to fit in. We went through the admission process and carried his few possessions to his room. He met his roommate, a young man named Doug who had a mild case of cerebral palsy.

The most interesting development came when I was about to leave and he followed me out to the car. A young woman walked over. She looked like she was in her early twenties. "What's your name?" she asked him.

"Medwin," he replied.

"Are you new?"

"Yeah."

"My name's Lucy. Do you want to be my boyfriend?"

"Okay," he agreed.

Apparently it was a done deal. I wondered about the implications of this relationship. Did Medwin know about sex? If his mother had been his sex ed instructor, I could only imagine the version of the birds and the bees she might have passed along. I decided we needed to have a little man-to-man talk before I left. "Medwin, I want to take you out to lunch," I said.

"Where?"

"McDonald's."

"Can I come?" his girlfriend of thirty seconds wanted to know.

"I think it would be better if just the two of us went, Lucy," I let her down gently. "Medwin and I have something we need to talk about."

"Okay," she said. She turned abruptly and marched off.

"I like her," Medwin decided.

"That's what we need to talk about."

On the way to McDonald's I stopped at a drug store and bought a box of condoms. When we were squared away in a booth with our Big Macs and fries I launched into the basics. I didn't quite know how to segue into the subject, so I jumped in feet first. "Medwin, has anyone ever talked with you about sex?"

"Uh huh," he said as he nibbled on his burger.

"Who?"

"Mama."

"What did she tell you?"

"Girls have eggs."

"That's right. And what happens to the eggs?"

"When they sit on them babies come out?" he took a stab at it.

125

"Not exactly." I grabbed a napkin and made a rough sketch of the female reproductive system, with ovaries and fallopian tubes. "Do you know what this is?"

He examined it curiously. "A goat's head?"

"It sort of looks like a goat, but it's a woman's insides. Do you know how a woman gets pregnant?"

He grinned shyly. "Yeah."

"How?"

"The man puts his wing dang doodle in the woman's fuzzy."

"Well, I've never heard it put quite that way, but you've got the basic idea. That's called having sex, right?"

"Some people call it fucking."

"Yep, same thing. It feels good, but the problem is sometimes a girl or a woman can get pregnant when she doesn't want to have a baby. Do you know how to keep a woman from getting pregnant?"

He shook his head.

I pulled a condom out of my pocket and showed it to him. "This is a condom – some people call it a rubber. You put it over your – uh, wing dang doodle – before you have sex and it protects the woman from getting pregnant. Some women take pills for the same reason, but this is how you can be extra sure." He stared at the mysterious little package. Out of the corner of my eye I could see the older couple in the booth across from us staring at it, too, so I laid it down quickly. "I've got more of these in the Jeep. I'll give you some before I go."

He was still trying to make sense of the little package. "It's square."

"No, no – that's just the wrapper. When you open it up it's shaped like a ... like a banana."

"Can I open it?"

I glanced at the couple and they diverted their eyes. "Sure, go on." He opened the package and examined the contents. "Go on, unroll it," I invited him.

McDonalds' menu has relatively few items that can be used to demonstrate the proper use of a condom. Inspired, I grabbed a handful of fries, squeezed them into something like mashed potatoes and shaped the greasy mess into an approximation of a hot dog. I placed it in front of him. "Okay, Medwin, go on and slide the condom over this."

The resulting mess looked like a Vienna sausage stuffed in a balloon, but it was close enough. "What's this little thing?" he pointed to the tip.

"That's the part that collects the semen that comes out of your penis - your wang dang doodle - and makes the woman pregnant."

"Oh."

"You know the stuff I'm talking about?"

"The white stuff?"

"Exactly."

I knew this lesson wasn't going to win any awards from the American Association of Sex Educators, Counselors and Therapists, but it served its purpose. I was feeling rather pleased with myself when I was suddenly aware of a man in a shirt and tie hovering over us.

"Excuse me," he said, looking uncomfortable. "I'm the manager. I had a complaint from a customer about, uh …" he pointed to the condom full of fries "…that."

"I'll throw it away," I offered quickly. I grabbed a couple of napkins, wrapped them around my little sculpture and dumped it in a nearby trashcan. "I was explaining the birds and the bees to my young friend," I told him.

"If you can find somewhere else to do it, we'd appreciate it."

"No problem."

"Why was he mad?" Medwin asked after he walked away.

"Some people are uncomfortable talking about sex."

"I'm not," he said.

"Good."

The next time I heard from Jack McManus he was back at work. True to his old form he showed up unannounced at the clinic and caught me between clients. He seemed a little slower and he'd lost a few pounds, but basically he was the same guy. "I don't want to interrupt you," he said apologetically. "I just want to say thanks for taking Medwin to Institute."

"My pleasure. How are you doing, Jack?"

"I'm fine, except I'm getting tired of telling everyone I'm fine."

"Okay, pretend I didn't ask. What's the latest on Medwin? How's he doing at Institute?"

He gave me a thumbs-up. "He's doing well. He'll probably finish up in two or three more months. He's even got a girlfriend."

"Lucy?"

"How'd you know?"

"They met the day I took him there."

"Apparently they're planning to get married."

"Very interesting. I hadn't heard that. Given their level of functioning, I hope they're up to the challenge."

"They had a little discipline problem with Medwin when he first got there," Jack revealed. "I think he was just trying to fit in by showing off. You know how kids are."

I found this curious since Medwin was a quiet, relatively shy young man. He didn't seem like a show-off. "What kind of discipline problem?" I wanted a little more information.

He suppressed a smile. "He decided to entertain the guys at his table in the cafeteria by squeezing a bunch of French fries into a replica of a cock. Then he stuck it in a rubber. Everyone in the cafeteria came over to inspect it. It caused quite a commotion."

"That's interesting," I said, shifting uncomfortably in my chair.

"These kids weren't raised like you and me, Greg," he reminded me. "They don't know the difference between appropriate and inappropriate social behavior. Some of them have grown up in unusual circumstances. You know what I mean. You've met Mrs. Bales."

"Did Medwin get in trouble for his little stunt?"

"Just a reprimand. What are you going to do about something like that except tell him its unacceptable behavior?"

"Given his relationship with Lucy it's nice to know he's aware of how to use a condom," I pointed out the bright side.

"I hadn't thought of it that way," he conceded. "I suppose you're right."

"You know what they always say, Jack. Better safe than sorry."

Chapter 18
Just a Suggestion

When you live in an area surrounded by natural beauty, you have your own favorite places, on and off the beaten path. My favorite spots aren't on the mountains and hills that afford sweeping panoramas of the Greenbrier Valley, but along the river that created it. When I'm kayaking and I reach a place I like, if the current is strong I'll pull into an eddy and linger, or if it's weak I'll stop paddling and let the kayak drift slowly downstream. Sometimes other paddlers appear, fishermen or kids from summer camps, but just as often the river is a private passage where your only companions are feathered or furry. I've watched hawks soaring along cliffs, heron fishing, flocks of ducks and Canada geese, whitetail deer, river otters, and a black bear and her cubs.

When I first moved to the valley one of my favorite public spots on the river was in the village of Fort Spring, halfway between Alderson and Lewisburg. P.K. and Betty Burdette owned a mom and pop store at a wide bend in the river, where the highway turns away and climbs a steep hill. The Burdettes had a grocery, a restaurant and a laundromat, and P.K. did a little gun trading on the side for good measure. On days when I felt too tired to fix my own meals, I'd grab dinner at their counter on the way home from work. Libby's father, Joe, was also a regular customer, but he usually stopped for lunch.

The Burdettes had four sons. Their youngest, Johnny, attended the state school for the deaf in Romney. I'd worked with deaf students before and I knew a little sign language. When Johnny was around I'd try to practice it, but he kept getting better, which made me look worse. I asked P.K. and Betty if I could write an article about Johnny for a regional magazine, using him to illustrate what it was like growing up deaf in the Mountain State. When the feature came out, they were pleased.

P.K. was aware that I'd been spending a lot of time with Joe's daughter, mainly because Libby and I were often in his store together. When I stopped by one evening in early December to scarf down one of Betty's cheeseburgers he moseyed over. "Are you still seeing Libby Meadows?"

"Yep," I said. "Three months now."

"Now there's the girl you should marry," he offered an unvarnished opinion. "She's got everything going for her."

"I know, I know," I said.

P.K.'s advice came as a surprise because no one had ever come right out before and told me I should get married. But I figured you only have three major decisions to make in life: where to live, who to live with, and what to do with your time. I'd found a line of work I liked and a place where I wanted to be. The last piece of the puzzle was finding someone to share the adventure.

I drove home along the river thinking about P.K.'s suggestion.

When I sleep, my dreams are usually nonsensical. I create exotic places that don't exist and I visit them repeatedly. I play instruments I can't play. In the bluest of moons I'll have one that has a little more substance. That night I dreamed I was interviewing Bob Dylan. I asked him which of his songs was his personal favorite. He didn't hesitate. "*Just Like a Woman*," he said. Then I asked him something no one had probably ever asked him before. "What line have you heard that you wish you could have written?"

He gave me an enigmatic Dylan look. "The heart is a lonely hunter," he replied.

The Heart is a Lonely Hunter is a 1940 novel by Carson McCullers, set in Georgia. The main character is a deaf man. Another one of the characters, Biff Brannon, is a restaurant owner who's very perceptive. I don't spend much time trying to interpret dreams, but this one seemed pretty obvious.

The next night I called Libby. "Want to go to the Court Restaurant and get some pie?"

"Sure," she said. She probably figured that on a social worker's salary I couldn't afford a whole meal.

I was planning to propose to her. I had decided to wait until we were on our way home and stop at some romantic spot along the river. I wasn't a get-down-on-my-knee-and-flash-a-diamond-ring kind of guy; it wouldn't have felt right for either of us. Besides, Libby had told me more than once that she didn't really care for diamonds. After we finished our cherry pie and were still talking, I decided there was no sense putting it off.

I looked into her blue eyes and smiled. "So when do you want to get married?"

She considered it briefly. "How about June?"

"I'm going to a social work conference at the University of Wisconsin in June," I told her. "I've got to be there because I'm presenting one of the workshops."

"Then how about May?" she moved it up a month.

"May's good," I said. "We both have birthdays in June and if were going to do this, we might as well do it while we're still young."

She agreed, and it was a done deal. Our relationship had been very comfortable from the beginning. Before we left the restaurant to celebrate and break the news to our families, there was something else we needed to discuss. Well, maybe one-and-a-half things.

"I've got an unusual job," I told her something she already knew. "Social workers don't usually deal with people who are joyously happy. Sometimes my clients and their problems are going to get in our way. I get lots of phone calls in the middle of the night."

"It's part of the package," she accepted it. "Doctors get phone calls in the middle of the night, too."

"Yeah, but doctors are well-compensated. If you marry a social worker, you're getting all the inconvenience and none of the money."

"The money doesn't matter."

She really felt that way. Her family was comfortably middle-class, but there was little evidence of impulse buying in the Meadows' home. They were careful with what they had. Like her parents, Libby didn't spend much time thinking about money or the things it could buy.

"There's also the matter of an Old English Sheepdog," I reminded her. "You're going to have to share me with a big furry creature who thinks he owns the place."

"I love Alfie," she insisted. "I'm marrying you for your dog."

"So he really is a babe magnet?"

"He's magnetized at least one."

Now that we had the rest of our lives worked out, we weren't in any big rush to leave the restaurant. We lingered over pie and coffee, trying to figure out how to break the news to our families.

"We want to come up and meet Libby," my mother reacted when I called Saturday night and told my parents there was going to be a wedding in May. I'd been living in West Virginia for two-and-a-half years and this was the first time my parents had mentioned visiting. I could already see that marriage was going to change a lot of things.

"You'll like her," I promised. "And Joe and Ruth, too. When do you want to come?"

"Next week," she surprised me. "Can you make a reservation for us for three nights at The Greenbrier? People have been telling us for years how wonderful it is."

"Sure, I'll call the hotel. This is going to be fun."

"Make a dinner reservation, too, and please invite Ruth and Joe."

"We haven't even told them we're getting married yet. Libby tried to get them to invite me over for dinner tonight, but Joe was shampooing the carpets and Ruth didn't want visitors while they were still wet. I've got a feeling if they knew what was going on they wouldn't be worrying about the carpets. We're planning to tell them tomorrow."

"Please make sure you invite them to dinner."

"Okay."

"How long have you known Libby?" my father was curious.

"Three months. We started dating in September."

"Three months?" From the tone of his voice I could hear him questioning this whirlwind romance. In his early days as a lawyer he'd handled his share of divorce cases. They were ugly messes and he hadn't liked the experience. He once observed that he'd lost a lot of friends by handling their divorces. He'd bailed out of that kind of practice years ago to specialize in labor law.

"We're not exactly youngsters," I reminded him. "Libby's 24. She also happens to be perfect."

"You found a perfect 24-year-old woman who hasn't been married before?"

"It's kind of hard to believe," I had to admit. "But once you get past her hunchback and eye patch you'll love her."

There was a brief silence on the other end of the line. My mother broke it. "You are kidding, aren't you?"

"You'll have to wait until next week and see for yourselves."

I'd logged a lot of time at the Meadows' home over the past several months, but on this particular Sunday they weren't up for visitors. Joe was worn out from 10 hours of cleaning carpets. Ruth wasn't feeling well and she'd let the family know she wasn't up to making their usual Sunday dinner. They planned to go to church, come home and grab a quick bite, and spend the afternoon napping in front of the TV. Libby was determined that we were going to tell her parents that we were engaged, no matter how they were feeling.

I asked her if Joe would expect me to ask his permission for his daughter's hand in marriage. "No, he's not like that," she said. "We just need to tell them."

She told her mother that she would make dinner. "When Dad finds out that I'm planning to grill steaks, he'll want to do it," she predicted. "I'll make everything else."

Sunday dinner came together and we broke them the news at their dining room table. They were thrilled. Our engagement had a curative effect. Joe recovered his energy and Ruth's illness went away. When they asked when and where we wanted to get married, I don't think they were expecting us to have a plan in place.

"In May," Libby told them. "Under the dogwood tree in the backyard."

They looked out the picture window, imagining the scene.

My parents fell in love with Libby, which was a given, and they hit it off well with Joe and Ruth. We invited Charlie and Marjorie Lobban over hoping the two lawyers would find lawyerly things to talk about. They talked about everything else, which probably worked out better. Anne Blair insisted on having them over for cocktails, and they bonded with my employer over bourbon and scotch in her grand home.

We squeezed in a visit to the Riverside Inn, a restaurant in Pence Springs that served Colonial cuisine in a candlelit log cabin. My mother decided it was a good place for our rehearsal dinner.

When the six of us had dinner at The Greenbrier, my parents discovered that Ruth was a local celebrity. She had been teaching food service and cooking classes at Greenbrier East High School for years. Many of her former students worked at the resort in the kitchen and as waitstaff. As we sat in the main dining room, a steady stream of people approached the table to say hello to Mrs. Meadows and let her know she had been their favorite teacher. Ruth was an exceptionally kind and sweet person, and it was easy to see why her students felt this way. As the years went on, I don't think we ever had a meal with Joe and Ruth at The Greenbrier that Ruth didn't get this kind of attention from the staff.

My parents had traveled quite a bit but they'd always gone the standard tourist route, staying in hotels filled with other tourists and seeing the usual sights. It would never have crossed their minds to wander the back streets, mix it up with the locals, or eat at funky restaurants. Their inaugural visit to West Virginia was a new experience for them because they were meeting the locals, and they weren't being treated like tourists, except at the hotel.

The day they left we decided they needed to experience something earthier than The Greenbrier's rarified atmosphere. Clingmans' Market on Washington Street in Lewisburg filled the bill. *Market* was a misnomer, because the place was really a tiny restaurant, disguised as a tiny grocery. It wasn't the kind of dining experience most tourists seek out. Gwen Clingman served up her country cooking from a stove in the back room for $2 a meal. The market was dark and dusty, and crammed with as many tables and chairs as she could fit in. Gwen wasn't running a standard food service operation and it was a miracle the health inspectors had never closed the place down. People suspected that she bribed them with free meals.

A write-up about Clingmans' Market once appeared in *Southern Living*. A woman who was staying at The Greenbrier read the article and thought the restaurant sounded quaint. She decided to entertain 5 of her friends by having a luncheon at Clingman's. She called Gwen and tried to make a reservation. Gwen explained that there weren't any reservations. As her caller became insistent, Gwen realized she didn't have any idea of what the restaurant was like. "Honey, you don't understand," she said to her. "This place is a dump." It wasn't the way most proprietors would have described their restaurants, but Gwen believed in brutal honesty.

We hit Gwen's on turkey day, which meant we had an approximation of Thanksgiving dinner. The place was bustling with professors and students from the West Virginia School of Osteopathic Medicine, and the more colorful locals included a couple of farmers in bib overalls. My parents had a kind of dining experience they'd never had in their travels. We were feeling generous and we picked up the check.

"West Virginia's more beautiful than I thought," my mother summed up her impressions as they left. "And the people are so warm and friendly." For the first time instead of questioning why their son had forsaken sunny Florida for this foreign land, they were starting to understand.

Chapter 19
A Good Peon

I checked the directions I'd been given and decided the canary-yellow house was the Family Refuge Center. Domestic violence shelters were a new concept, and the Refuge had only recently opened. Women trying to escape abusive partners often faced limited options, and shelters like the Refuge offered a safe haven and support while the victims regrouped. I parked in front of the house and rang the doorbell. A woman with a ponytail cracked the door and eyed me cautiously.

"Are you Greg?" she asked.

"Yes," I said. "Anne Blair said you needed some help."

She unlatched the chain and let me in. "We'd appreciate it if you'd keep our location confidential."

"Sure. How's business?"

"We've been open three months and we've had 17 clients." I followed her through the living room, which was furnished with cargo-style furniture, and into the office. She closed the door. "We've got an awkward situation," she confided. "Last night we took in our first man. His wife threatened him at gunpoint and fired shots at him. He's just as much a victim as the women here, but they're uncomfortable having a man in the house. We're not really set up for males."

"Are the police involved?"

"He's afraid to go to the police. We've got to get him out of here. He's not a problem. He has impeccable manners. In fact, he's charming."

"You make it sound like you want us to adopt a cute pet," I teased her.

"And there's no adoption fee," she sweetened the pot. "Can you take him with you?"

The clinic was an extension of Anne Blair's instinctive hospitality, so I knew the answer she'd expect me to give. "Sure, we can take him. I don't know what we're going to do with him once we do."

"Thanks. We owe you."

We would undoubtedly collect. Decades before the business community fell in love with the term networking, social service agencies were constantly trading favors great and small. I left the shelter in the company of Manius Treadwell, a dapper little black man in his early sixties who spoke with a Caribbean lilt.

"Where are you from, Manius?" I asked him. "Jamaica?"

"Close, Mr. Johnson," he replied. "I'm from the Abaco Islands."

"Where's that?"

"The Abacos are on the northern end of the Bahamas. I grew up in a little town called Marsh Harbor. I left many years ago, but they tell me I still have a touch of the patois."

"I'm not sure what a patois is, but I like the way you talk."

"My clients always comment about it."

"What sort of clients do you have?"

"I have a limousine service, Debonair Limo. I just have the one car, but it pays the bills."

"Sounds like a good way to make a living."

"I'm just a peon, Mr. Johnson," he said humbly. "But a good peon can make a good living. I have some faithful clients and I get some very nice tips."

"You own a limo and I'm chauffeuring you?"

He sighed. "Last night when I was leaving for work, Ivy shot out my tires. She carries a little pearl-handled pistol in her handbag. She claims it's for self-protection, but she uses it to terrorize me. Her aim is getting better all the time. I believe she must be taking target practice somewhere."

"That sounds pretty serious."

"It is serious! I fear for my life! I need a hiding place. Will you help me?"

"I'd rather help you find a solution to your problems."

He shook his head sadly. "I'm afraid there are no solutions, Mr. Johnson."

"Please call me Greg. Or is that against the Peon Code?"

"I'm more comfortable calling you Mr. Johnson."

"Everyone calls me Greg. It's not a cool name like Manius, but I'm used to it."

"It just doesn't seem proper to call you Greg."

"Okay, just for you I'll be Mr. Johnson. How long have you been married?"

"I've been with Ivy for 35 years now. I'm not looking forward to the thirty-sixth year, but she threatens to have me deported if I leave her."

"How could she have you deported?"

"I came to this country illegally, Mr. Johnson. I don't have a Social Security card and I've never paid income taxes. I've gotten away with it because I'm self-employed."

"Is Ivy a U.S. citizen?"

"Yes. Ivy grew up in Ronceverte."

"I don't know much about the immigration laws, but doesn't marrying a U.S. citizen automatically qualify you for citizenship?"

"Yes, but there's a little hitch. We present ourselves as husband and wife and we have four children, but we've never married."

"Don't 35 years and four kids count for something?"

"Common law marriages aren't recognized in West Virginia," he educated me. "I've discussed it with lawyers and they all tell me the same thing. I'm in a terrible pickle, Mr. Johnson. My home phone is my work phone. That's how my clients reach me. I won't have any work if I don't go home."

"Are you really afraid of Ivy?"

"Yes!"

We arrived at the clinic and I took Manius Treadwell up to my office and opened a case file on him. I was impressed to learn that he'd put three of his children through college, and his fourth was at Marshall

University. He should have been proud of his accomplishments, but he was too upset to be proud of anything.

Anne Blair sent me to the ministerial association to solicit funds for emergency housing. I installed Manius in a drab little room in a motel on the outskirts of town. I left him there and went to call on Ivy the Terrible.

Nothing about Ivy Treadwell fit the pistol-packin' mama image. She was dressed stylishly and she comported herself with matronly dignity. Her toy poodle Nikki pranced into the living room, hopped up on the sofa and made herself at home. Nikki's updo and bejeweled collar suggested she was a pampered pooch. The house was well kept, and photos of the children were everywhere. If I hadn't seen a limousine with four flattened tires sitting in the driveway, I would have doubted my client's version of things.

"I won't take up much of your time, Ms. Treadwell," I got right to the point. "Manius is afraid to come home. We've given him temporary housing and we're trying to help him sort things out."

"Oh poo," she said with a dismissive wave of her hand. "Manius can come home any time he wants. He knows that."

"He said you shot out his tires."

She rolled her eyes, accented by mascara-thickened lashes and smoky eye shadow. "We just had a little tiff. Manius loves to make mountains out of molehills."

"It sounds like this molehill involved gunfire. Do you own a gun?"

"Yes," she admitted. "Manius works nights and I'm here alone. Our son Antoine gave me a little purse pistol for self-protection."

"Your husband is scared of it."

"Manius is scared of his own shadow. It's just a little .22. It wouldn't hurt a flea."

"Mrs. Treadwell, even if it's 'just a little .22', if someone fired shots at me I'd be nervous, too. Do you have a permit for it?" Her polite veneer faded; I realized that now I was sounding more like a cop than a social worker. In West Virginia the right to bear arms ranks right up there with life, liberty, beans and cornbread. Our Supreme Court justices probably packed heat under their robes. "I'm sorry," I backpedaled. "I can see that question bothered you."

I was shifting to active listening, a counseling technique where you ignore the facts and focus on feelings. It works well when you want to keep someone talking. I taught it to my friend Martin who anchors a local news broadcast and he says he uses it when he conducts interviews. "It's amazing what people will tell you if they think you're a sympathetic listener," he observes.

"You're acting like I'm some kind of common criminal," she accused me. "Don't you think a mother who raised four high achievers deserves a little respect?"

"Yes, you certainly do. Manius told me about your children. I know you're proud of them." She'd already told me in so many words that she was, so I was just focusing on her feelings of pride.

She launched into a litany of the Treadwell offsprings' miraculous accomplishments. I smiled and nodded, but she didn't need any encouragement. When she finally paused, I jumped in.

"It must be quite an adjustment for you now that your children are gone." Her eyes watered and I knew I'd hit on something. She'd been a mother hen and her chicks had flown the coop. I asked a few more questions and discovered that she was bored being at home by herself while Manius drove all over the countryside. The disabled vehicle in the driveway was an illustration of her feelings on the matter. "Mrs. Treadwell, have you ever heard of Empty Nest Syndrome?"

"I've heard something about it," she said.

"You think you might have it?"

"Sometimes I sit in their bedrooms and cry my eyes out. I know it's silly, but I just can't help it."

She'd been a stay-at-home mom all her life and now she'd lost her sense of purpose. She wasn't a churchgoer, she didn't belong to clubs and she didn't do volunteer work, so she didn't have much to fill the vacuum. "Have you ever thought about getting a job?" I suggested.

She made a face and I could see the idea didn't sit well. "What would I do? Work at a convenience store? Sell shoes and handbags in one of those tourist shops at The Greenbrier? Sell encyclopedias door to door? Those things are a little below my station in life, don't you think? We're business *owners*, not someone's *employees*."

Her haughty attitude contrasted sharply with Manius's humble nature. I thought about suggesting marriage counseling, but I didn't think Ivy would buy it. It was time to put the ball back in Manius's court.

We sat on the edge of his bed at the motel and reviewed my home visit. "Ivy's bored and lonely," I shared my impressions. "She doesn't know what to do with herself now that the kids are gone. She's taking it out on you because you're handy and you're enjoying a kind of freedom she doesn't have."

"Maybe that's true, Mr. Johnson," he admitted, "but nothing's stopping Ivy from pursuing other interests. The fact of the matter is she doesn't have any. She never has."

"Put yourself in her shoes, Manius. She's sitting alone at home every night, flipping through TV channels and stewing in her own juices while you're out meeting interesting people and driving all over creation."

"I wish I could stay home," he said. "Sometimes I get tired of smiling at people, especially when they're being obnoxious. But what can I do? Driving is my livelihood. I can't stay home just to keep Ivy company. We couldn't pay the bills and then we'd both be out on the street. She wouldn't be happy with that arrangement either."

"I'm pretty sure Empty Nest Syndrome is the root of your problem, Manius, unless there's something else you haven't told me. You're not running around on Ivy, are you?"

His eyes grew a big as saucers. "Would you cheat on a woman with a bad temper and a gun?"

"No, I don't believe I would."

"I don't know what Antoine was thinking when he gave her that thing. She used to be irritating. Now she's armed and dangerous. She has no business with a handgun."

I didn't want to become their family diplomat, shuttling back and forth between the two of them, trying to hammer out a shaky peace agreement. "I agree," I said. "I'm all for empowering women, but not with bullets. You've got to get that thing away from her."

"Me! She'd shoot me! I suppose I could have her arrested, but then she'd take her revenge out on me when they let her out." He put his head in his hands, a defeated man. "I'm not thinking very clearly, Mr. Johnson. I barely slept last night. I just don't know what to do."

"I've got an idea that might be worth a shot."

He peeked at me through his splayed fingers. "What?"

Three weeks later I was in my office when Jayne buzzed on the intercom and asked me to come downstairs. I expected to find someone who needed help negotiating the stairs, but Manius was standing in the front hallway, decked out in his uniform.

"You cut a dashing figure, Manius."

"Thank you, Mr. Johnson. They say clothes make the man."

"I hope it's not true. Even expensive clothes look cheap on me."

"Now, now," he wagged an admonishing finger. "You mustn't be so hard on yourself."

"So you're back at work now?"

"Yes, I am. If you can come outside with me I'd like to show you something."

His limousine was idling on the street in front of the building. Ivy was behind the wheel, looking chic in her own chauffeur's uniform. She gave me a regal wave. "Hello, Mr. Johnson. Would you like to go for a little ride? I'll have you back in five minutes."

"Sure. I've never been in a limo before."

Manius held the door and I climbed in. He took a seat next to me and Ivy pulled away from the curb. We passed Old Stone Church and headed up the hill to the Confederate Cemetery, where 95 soldiers were laid to rest in a mass grave. We looped around and continued out to Route 60, where a steep hill descended back into town. Like many mothers, Ivy had been a chauffeur for years, driving her children all over creation. She hadn't been behind the wheel of a limo, but she handled the vehicle with confidence.

"Can she hear us?" I asked Manius.

"Not when the glass is closed," he said. "Your little idea worked like a charm. She looks smart in her uniform, too."

I'd hit on the notion when I was thinking about her statement that "we" were business owners, not "someone's employee". If she considered herself the co-owner of the company, why not let her participate?

"We took care of the problem with the pistol, too," he confided. "Antoine convinced her to give it back to him. I didn't think she'd cooperate, but he told us we're going to be grandparents. That softened her up considerably."

"Between chauffeuring and grandmothering she should be busy."

"Yes, and this way I get some nights. I can have a little peace and quiet at home when she's working." As we pulled up in front of the clinic a couple on the sidewalk on the other side of the street gawked. "When you arrive in a limousine with a driver, people think you're somebody," Manius explained with a twinkle in his eye.

"Let's have some fun," I proposed. I took out my Ray-Bans and slipped them on. Manius caught on and played along. He hopped out, opened the door with a flourish and stood at attention as I emerged, looking self-important. I wished Ivy good luck with her new career and I hurried into the clinic.

I hurried upstairs to my office, which overlooked the street. I could hear the couple pumping Manius for information.

"Just tell us if he's someone famous," the woman begged him.

Manius remained tight-lipped. "I'm afraid I'm not at liberty to say," he replied.

Her husband pointed to the clinic's sign. "Hell, he's probably just some screwed-up rock star with a drug problem. I bet he trashed his room at The Greenbrier and they shipped his butt over here."

Manius gave them an inscrutable smile. He walked around to the vehicle's passenger side and climbed into the front seat with Ivy. As suddenly as he'd come into my life, my favorite peon disappeared around the corner.

Chapter 20
The Interrogation

Once upon a time county jails reflected the personalities of the sheriffs who ran them. More than a few resembled the congenial lockup Andy Taylor and Barney Fife operated in Mayberry. But the hometown hoosegow has pretty much become a thing of the past, replaced by uninviting regional fortresses wrapped in razor wire. Aunt Bee doesn't drop by with blackberry cobbler.

The Greenbrier County jail used to be a place where drunks could sleep off their hangovers, vagrants could grab a night of lodging, and joyriding juveniles would cool their heels under the same roof as adults. From time to time we would get a call at the clinic reporting that one of the county guests was behaving a little oddly - "he just ain't right" was the operative phrase - and we'd go over and size things up.

This time the call came from a lawyer. I hadn't met Ed King, but he had a sterling reputation. If you were down and out and needed legal help, Ed was your guy. Unlike some other court-appointed lawyers, whose hearts were in real estate or personal injury, Ed knew criminal law and he'd give you a defense that was often better than you deserved. He collected minimal pay from the public coffers, but this didn't seem to bother him. He was the equivalent of a public defender before the county had a defender's office.

"I'm representing a 17-year-old named Elmo Beane," he said over the phone. "He stole a car in Fairlea. They picked him up in

Huntington going the wrong way on a one-way street. I can't get anything out of this kid. I think he's depressed. I'm afraid he might be suicidal. Will you guys evaluate him?"

"I'll talk with him," I offered. "Then we'll probably ask the deputies to bring him over to see Dr. Ableman."

"Oh, there's one other thing," he added like Lieutenant Columbo. "They found the body of the owner of the car he took behind the livestock market in Caldwell. A man named Bailey. He died from blunt trauma to the head. The kid claims he doesn't know anything about it. He says he saw the car with the keys in it in front of the guy's trailer and he took it."

"Do you believe him?"

"I don't know. Like I say, he won't talk much."

"Does he have a family?"

"A mother and sister. They live in the same trailer park as the victim."

"What would you like us to do?"

"Get him out of there and into a psych unit where they can keep an eye on him."

I walked over to the county jail, which was next door to the courthouse. One of the deputies escorted a pale young man in jeans and a T-shirt into the interview room and left us alone. Elmo Beane was the kind of guy you'd pass a hundred times in your high school hall and never noticed - brown eyes, brown hair, average height and build – just another face in the crowd. The dark circles under his eyes suggested that he hadn't been sleeping much. I introduced myself and explained that his lawyer had asked me to talk with him. He didn't reply.

"Do you go to Greenbrier East?" I kept it simple.

He shook his head.

"Did you graduate?"

He shook it again.

"School wasn't your thing?"

He shrugged.

"Where'd you go to grade school?"

"Ronceverte."

Getting an uncommunicative person to talk is like starting a lawn mower in the spring. You pull the cord and at first there's no response. You keep trying and you start to hear a little cough. After ten more pulls, if you haven't flooded the engine or given up, the mower slowly rumbles to life.

When Elmo finally rumbled to life he told me about his absent father, his mother who was having a hard time making ends meet, and how he'd grown up in the community without ever feeling like he was part of it. He had a learning problems and apparently his brain wasn't wired for reading. As a result he'd spent his school days helping the maintenance man while his classmates plodded through textbooks and labored over essays. Social promotions carried him through the elementary grades but came to a screeching halt in high school. He dropped out when he turned sixteen.

One thing he had learned in school was how to play the guitar. The maintenance man kept a beat-up instrument in the basement, and when he wasn't busy mopping up spills in the cafeteria or tinkering with the furnace, he taught Elmo to play. He'd given him the guitar when he left grade school.

"So how good are you?" I asked him.

"I can play Black Mountain Rag."

"Then you're better than me." A flicker of a smile crossed his face, so I stuck with the topic of music. While his friends were listening to the Eagles and Bob Marley and Pink Floyd, his buddy had introduced him to bluegrass. I asked Elmo if he played in a band.

"My guitar's not good enough," he said. "I was savin' up for one and then dad showed up and borrowed all my money. We ain't seen him since."

"Tough break."

"I hate his guts."

I gestured at the green walls. "So how'd you get yourself into this fix, Elmo?"

He looked at the floor. "That old bastard had the hots for my sister."

I had a hunch I knew who the old bastard was. "How old is your sister?"

"Twelve."

"How old was the old bastard?"

"Like seventy or somethin'."

"That's not good."

"He had a picture of her right by his bed, in a frame and everythin'."

"Where'd he get it?"

"She give it to him."

"Sounds like a dirty old man."

He kept his eyes on the floor. "Not no more."

I left with Elmo's permission to share what he'd told me with his lawyer. Ed King's modest office was on the next block. I told his secretary it was urgent and she led me into his inner sanctum, cluttered with papers and files. "Your boy just confessed to murder," I broke him the news. "I told him you needed to know the truth so you can figure out the best way to defend him."

He looked surprised. "You must be one hell of an interrogator."

His use of the word interrogator threw me. "I didn't interrogate him, Ed. We were just talking. Once he got comfortable, he slipped it into the conversation matter-of-factly. I think he needed to get it off his chest and I just happened to be the person who was there. The kid's hardly slept since it happened. Apparently the victim was a pedophile who had the hots for his 12-year-old sister. Elmo claims he'd been plying her with booze and pot."

"Was it premeditated?"

"I don't know the legal definition of premeditated. He went over to the guy's trailer to confront him about his sister. Bailey tried to calm him down with Wild Turkey. They started drinking and eventually Bailey passed out in his chair. Elmo went home and came back with a baseball bat and bashed him in the head."

"Was he drunk?"

"I don't know. If he was, Bailey was the one who got him that way."

"You say he gave alcohol to the sister too?"

"Yep. According to Elmo he had his eye on all the young girls in the park."

"This is great stuff," he said with enthusiasm. He wasn't applauding pedophilia or the murder, of course. He was celebrating what a defense lawyer always hopes for in a homicide, an unsympathetic victim and a sympathetic defendant.

"When he realized he'd killed the guy he panicked," I continued the story. "He stuffed the body in the trunk of his car, drove him to the stockyard, threw him over the hill and kept driving. They stopped him in Huntington for a traffic violation and they discovered he didn't have a driver's license and he couldn't explain where he'd gotten someone else's car."

"What did he do with the murder weapon?"

"He tossed it in the Kanawha River when he drove over the bridge at St. Albans. If bats float, I guess it could be in the Ohio by now, en route to the Mississippi. He vacuumed and cleaned the trunk at a car wash, so there probably isn't much evidence. He says there wasn't any blood."

King nodded thoughtfully. "It fits the facts. Bailey died of intracerebral hematoma."

"Now that Elmo's confessed, I don't think he's much of a suicide risk," I offered an opinion. "But you need to get over there right away and let him tell you the story. He needs to know you're on his side and you'll try to defend him."

"We're talking a plea, not a trial," he said. "He'll serve some time. But given his age and the circumstances and the fact that he's cooperating, we've got something to work with. Can you give him something to help him sleep?"

"I'll ask Dr. Ableman. Just ask them to bring him over to the clinic when you're done with him." He followed me to the door.

"Great job, man," he clapped me on the back. "You must be a really good interrogator."

"I didn't interrogate him," I insisted again. "We just talked. I don't know the first thing about interrogations."

"Apparently you know more than you think," he said, and we left it at that.

Virginia McLaughlin, who retired as the warden of the federal prison in Alderson, told my social work students that she'd rather have a murderer clean her office than a thief. "Most murderers are murderers one day in their lives," she said in her typical blunt fashion "A thief is a thief from the day he's born to the day he dies. You can't trust a thief. They'll look you in the eye and lie to you and swear to God it's the truth." Now I saw her point. Elmo was the first killer I'd ever met, but I didn't feel uncomfortable being with him. He wasn't creepy or calculating. He'd just had a bad day. A really, really bad day.

An investigation turned up other young girls in the trailer park who'd been propositioned by Bailey. He wasn't going to be sorely missed in the neighborhood. Ed King arranged for Elmo to plead to involuntary manslaughter. He was sentenced to 1-5 years at Anthony Correctional Center, a state facility for youthful offenders. He was a compliant inmate and he earned his release in three years.

The Beanes moved away and Elmo vanished from my radar. He's probably living a quiet, unassuming life somewhere, with his next-door neighbors blissfully unaware that once upon a time the guy strumming his guitar on the front porch was a murderer.

Chapter 21
A Placebo Exorcism

By their very nature mental health facilities are prone to strange episodes. One of our strangest began innocently enough one winter afternoon when Father Andy and I were sitting in his office talking about the WVU basketball team. Anne Blair came in, looking exhausted. She plopped down in a chair.

"Rough day?" Father Andy gathered.

She let out a sigh. "I've been with a 46-year-old woman who thinks she's possessed by the devil. She's convinced demons have taken over her body. She's a little vague about how they got there."

I thought of Linda Blair in *The Exorcist*. "Is she levitating?"

"Not yet. I talked to Pete and he said it could be hysteria, schizophrenia, multiple personality, or just plain old attention-getting." She looked at Father Andy questioningly. "Is it possible for someone to be possessed?"

"Back in Biblical times everyone believed in it," he reacted. "They didn't have any scientific knowledge, so they blamed everything on evil spirits - birth defects, seizures, mental illness. Some cultures still think that way. She's not from Haiti or the Philippines is she?"

"No, she's from Frankford. She claims she hears voices telling her she's damned. Her husband says she has violent outbursts whenever she sees a crucifix. She growls and curses. He took her to the emergency room and they couldn't find anything wrong with her, so they sent her to us."

"What's her religious background?" Father Andy wondered.

"Roman Catholic. Her husband says she used to go to church every time the doors were open. He accused her of having a crush on the priest and she stopped going."

"Maybe she's trying to get back at him," I tossed out a suggestion.

"No, I think this lady really believes she's possessed."

"Could be guilt," Father Andy hypothesized. "Maybe she had the hots for her priest and she thinks God's upset with her."

"We could probably get that part sorted out in therapy," Anne Blair ventured. "But I can't work with her the way she is."

"I could perform an exorcism," Father Andy offered.

We looked at him.

"A *placebo* exorcism," he clarified things. "A spiritual sugar pill. We can exorcize her delusions. I can take her over to the church, light some candles and command her evil spirits to leave."

"Wouldn't you need your bishop's permission?" Anne Blair asked him.

"If I asked the bishop's permission to perform a fake exorcism he'd think I'm nuts. You go with whatever works. This might."

"In *The Exorcist* the devil threw the priest down stairs and killed him," I reminded him.

"We just re-carpeted the sanctuary," he reacted. "At least I'll have a soft landing."

Like most progressive clergymen Father Andy didn't interpret the Bible literally. He saw possession as more of a Hollywood preoccupation than a modern day reality. I was squarely in his corner. "I'll be your altar boy," I volunteered.

"Seriously?"

"Sure. I used to be one. All I have to do is light the candles and stand there and hand you stuff. I don't want to miss it."

"When would you want to do it?" Anne Blair asked him.

"How about Friday afternoon?"

"I'll explain what we're thinking to her husband," she decided. "We'll see how he feels about it."

I tried to imagine this conversation. "I'd love to be a fly on the wall in your office. 'Well, sir, what we want to do is perform a fake exorcism on your wife.' "

"He'll go along with it," she predicted. "He's at his wit's end."

"Desperate times call for desperate placebos," Father Andy said.

I remembered a story from one of my psychology textbooks that seemed to fit the situation. The writer described a creative approach he liked to use with clients who complained of insomnia. He would instruct them to make a cup of hot chocolate, get two vanilla wafers (no more, no less – the number was important), and make themselves comfortable in bed. They were to slowly sip the hot chocolate and eat the cookies. He was amazed at the number of people who told him how well this worked. He was amazed because he'd made the whole thing up. He was relying on the power of suggestion. Humans are highly suggestible; if we weren't, there wouldn't be a zillion dollar advertising industry.

I viewed Father Andy's approach as a variation on the hot chocolate-and-cookies treatment, except demonic possession was a lot more interesting than insomnia.

We were waiting in the church sanctuary. Father Andy was vested in a white surplice and purple stole, and he'd outfitted me with a layreader's robe and cincture. We'd lit every candle we could find and we had a little bucket of fake holy water.

"I've learned more about exorcism in the last three days than I did in three years at the seminary," he told me. "The Episcopal Church has a prescribed ritual but they don't make it available to parish priests. Every diocese is supposed to have an exorcist appointed by the bishop and the exorcist is the one who has access to the ritual. The Catholic Church has a long rite with prayers, psalms, litanies, scripture readings and an exorcism you chant until the demon leaves. I've adapted the Catholic version and cut it down."

"Do you see any psychological danger in doing this?" I asked him.

"I've thought about it. The only danger I see is if it doesn't work. She might think God has abandoned her and she could turn depressed or suicidal. I talked about it with Anne Blair. She said she'd rather deal with someone who's depressed than someone who's obsessed. Depression's easier to treat."

The church door opened and Anne Blair ushered a middle-aged couple into the vestibule. The woman put up a mild struggle as they steered her to the front of the church by her elbows. Superhuman strength was supposed to be a hallmark of possession, but she wasn't displaying it.

"Ramona, this is Father Andy," Anne Blair introduced them.

Ramona eyed the priest and started mumbling and cursing under her breath.

Father Andy took her hands in his own and said gently, "Ramona, we understand what you're going through and we're going to try to help you. Do you want to be free of your demons?"

"NO!" she barked in a deep voice.

"Yes, she does," her husband said.

"I know why you can't answer that question," Father Andy intuited. "Satan is controlling you and he doesn't want to leave your body. That was Satan saying no, wasn't it?"

"Yessss," she hissed like a snake.

"Okay, Ramona, what I want you to do is kneel down at the altar rail. I'm going to say some prayers, bless you with holy water and make the sign of the cross on your forehead three times. Then I'm going to command the evil spirits to leave your body. Do you understand?"

"Gaudicaca bronocasta," she said in a loud voice. "Sibolay sibolay sibolay."

"She's talking in another language," her husband explained.

I had my own opinion. "I don't think it's a language," I said to him. "It sounds more like she's speaking in tongues, like they do in some churches."

Anne Blair helped Ramona to her knees. Father Andy opened the ceremony by invoking Saint Michael the Archangel, who according to Christian and Jewish tradition had vanquished Satan and his minions to hell.

"Glorious St. Michael the Archangel, prince of heavenly armies, defend us in our battle against the forces of evil. Come to the assistance of Ramona Blankenship, whom God has created in his likeness, and be her guardian and protector. Take hold of Satan and bind him, that he may no longer hold her captive."

It might have been a placebo exorcism, but it sounded like the real deal to me.

"We're going to say a litany together," he told us. "I'll read the invocations and your response is 'Deliver us, O Lord.' "

From all sin,	*deliver us, O Lord.*
From your wrath,	*deliver us, O Lord.*
From sudden death,	*deliver us, O Lord.*
From the snares of the devil,	*deliver us, O Lord.*
From anger, hatred, and all ill will,	*deliver us, O Lord.*
From all lewdness,	*deliver us, O Lord.*
From lightning and tempest,	*deliver us, O Lord.*
From the scourge of earthquakes,	*deliver us, O Lord.*
From plague, famine, and war,	*deliver us, O Lord.*
From everlasting death,	*deliver us, O Lord.*
By the mystery of your holy incarnation,	*deliver us, O Lord.*
By your coming,	*deliver us, O Lord.*
By your birth,	*deliver us, O Lord.*
By your baptism and holy fasting,	*deliver us, O Lord.*
By your cross and passion,	*deliver us, O Lord.*
By your death and burial,	*deliver us, O Lord.*
By your holy resurrection,	*deliver us, O Lord.*
By the coming of the Holy Spirit,	*deliver us, O Lord.*
On the Day of Judgment,	*deliver us, O Lord.*

I don't know if it was because she'd been participating in this kind of rote prayer from early childhood, but Ramona was saying the responses. Whatever was going on with her, it wasn't demonic possession. Possessed people don't chant litanies at altar rails.

Father Andy reached for his Bible and flipped to a page he'd marked with a ribbon. "A reading from the Gospel of Luke," he introduced it. "At that time the seventy-two returned in high spirits. 'Master,' they said, 'even the demons are subject to us because we use your name!' 'Yes,' He said to them, 'I was watching Satan fall like lightning that flashes from heaven. But mind: it is I that have given you the power to tread upon serpents and scorpions, and break the dominion of the enemy everywhere; nothing at all can injure you. Just the same, do not rejoice in the fact that the spirits are subject to you, but rejoice in the fact that your names are engraved in heaven.' "

Ramona was going along with the ritual. If Hollywood had scripted the scene, her head would have been spinning around and she would have been projectile vomiting.

Father Andy asked for the bucket of holy water and he sprinkled some on her. He took his thumb and traced the sign of the cross three times on her forehead. "May God the Father, God the Son and God the Holy Spirit protect you." He moved on to the exorcism ritual, reading from a paper he'd tucked in his prayer book.

"I cast you out, unclean spirit! Begone and stay far from this creature of God! For He who once stilled the sea and the wind and the storm commands you. Tremble in fear, Satan, you robber of life, you corrupter of justice, you source of all evil. Begone in the name of the Father and of the Son and of the Holy Spirit! Repel, O Lord, the devil's power and put him to flight! Protect your servant Ramona and strengthen her." He placed a hand on the top of her head and commanded, "Begone, Satan!"

Ramona collapsed in a little pile at the altar rail. Anne Blair and her husband sprang forward and helped her to a pew where she could sit down.

"I think it worked," Ramona said breathlessly.

It wasn't the kind of religious service that made you want to chitchat over coffee and cookies when it was over. Ramona and her husband thanked Father Andy. Anne Blair gave him a nod, and she escorted the couple out of the church.

This was the most dramatic thing I'd witnessed since I started working at the clinic, not to mention the most creative. "Wow," was all I could say.

Father Andy smiled. "Remember, I'm a professional," he said. "Don't try this at home."

Chapter 22
Ugly Fred

For many years Greyhound operated an East-West route that snaked across West Virginia's southern mountains. Lewisburg's bus station was located near the town's crossroads, where U.S. 219 and 60 intersect. The bus depot had a lunch counter with a name that invited wisecracks, Terminal Lunch. Passengers would straggle in to grab a bite, and the occasional straggler would fail to get back on the bus. Sooner or later most of these rubber tramps ended up on the mental health clinic's doorstep. This was how Ugly Fred rolled into town.

Fred was taken by our fair city's charms, and he made the rounds of the pastors and social service agencies exploring his options. He didn't buy the old saw about beggars not being choosers. He was looking for an all-inclusive package with food, clothing, shelter and a little pocket money to boot. Someone had told him the clinic operated a home for recovering substance abusers, so he introduced himself as an alcoholic struggling to stay on the wagon. Hank gave him a brief assessment, then I drove him up to the Fellowship Home, an old pink house tucked in the woods above town. Fred was impressed with his new digs. "Very nice," he said as he gave the pantry a cursory inspection. "I think this is a good place to get myself back together."

"I'll see you in my office in the morning," I said. "We'll go over your history and open up a file."

He gave me a wary look. "My history?"

"We need some background information on you, Fred. This is a treatment program. We need to help you come up with a plan to address your problems."

"My biggest problem is that I need a place to live," he preferred to see it in simpler terms. "You've taken care of that."

"We're here to help you deal with your drinking. That's why we have a Fellowship Home."

"How is it a fellowship if I'm the only fellow?"

"Sometimes we've got four or five people living here and sometimes we don't have any. Right now it's a fellowship of one, but that could change any time. It doesn't cost anything to live here. All we ask is that you participate in treatment."

"I don't need any more treatment. I've had enough."

"You must have some underlying issues that explain why you've ended up here."

"I think my underlying issue's pretty obvious."

"Maybe it is to you, but it's not to me."

"Hah! All you counselor types are the same. Humor the poor bastard. Act like he's perfectly normal."

"How am I humoring you?"

"Did you forget your glasses today?"

"What should I be seeing?"

"I don't want your pity. I just want somewhere I can forget about my deformity without having to drink myself to death. Is that too much to ask?"

"Your ... deformity?"

"Don't give me that bullshit. I've heard it a thousand times. 'Oh, Mr. Walker, there's nothing wrong with the way you look, you're just imagining things.' Yeah, right. The Elephant Man was imagining things, too. So was Frankenstein."

I studied him more carefully, looking for some physical abnormality. He had some male pattern baldness going on, and his cheeks were doing the middle-aged sagging thing, where gravity sends fat deposits down and makes creases that weren't there before, but I didn't see anything out of the ordinary. Fred wasn't going to be fielding any phone calls from modeling agencies, but he looked like the average Joe. He would have passed unnoticed on any street in

North America. I was curious about all this. "What do you see when you look in the mirror?"

"Don't rub it in. It's bad enough that I have to live with it."

"If you think your appearance is a problem, we'll have to talk about it sooner or later."

"What are you going to do - get me plastic surgery?"

I smiled. "You never know."

"Too risky," he ruled it out. "But you might be able to help me get disability."

"I'm not sure they give disability for looks. I'll check it out. In the meanwhile enjoy your new home and I'll see you in the morning."

Drifters are usually running from something - relationships, responsibilities, or maybe just a chronic inability to keep it all together. No matter how fast or how far they run, their problems have a way of tagging along. This was certainly true in Fred's case. He claimed he'd always been deeply ashamed of his looks. While this might have spurred someone else to become Mr. Overachiever or Mr. Personality, Fred had hit the road. When I asked if he considered himself a bum, he was insulted. Bums are stationary, he explained. He was a vagabond. It had a carefree, devil-may-care ring that didn't seem to fit him.

The residents in our Fellowship Home worked with our substance abuse counselor, but Hank resisted dealing with Fred. "This guy's drinking because he thinks he's ugly," he said as he dropped his file back on my desk. "Ugly's your department. You cure that and then I'll take care of his drinking problem." He was out the door before I could protest.

Fred presented an intriguing challenge, a therapeutic Mount Everest. A parade of counselors, psychiatrists, psychologists and social workers had attempted to help him without any success. He was from Chillicothe, Ohio, and he claimed his parents had always favored his siblings. During his teenage years he took a long look in the mirror and decided the reason: he was a freak of nature. "My hairline looks like Herman Munster's," he said. "My nose belongs on a camel. My ears stick out. My teeth are crooked. My smile looks phony. My Adam's apple looks like I've got a Granny Smith stuck in my throat. I don't wear shorts because I don't want people making fun of my chicken legs."

I'd heard that when women look in mirrors they see only their flaws, but when men look in mirrors they're convinced they're only six more sit-ups away from a date with a supermodel. This definitely wasn't the case with Fred, who could only focus on a long list of imperfections that seemed like somatic delusions.

After high school he'd worked a series of low-wage restaurant jobs out of the public eye. He didn't pursue relationships because he thought women were repulsed by his grotesque appearance. He took up drinking as a consolation and he made a pleasant discovery: some women would have sex with him if they were drunk enough. This led him to spending a lot of time in bars. Eventually alcohol got the better of him and he couldn't even hold menial jobs, so he threw himself on the mercy of the social service system. When social workers and counselors grew tired of him in one place he'd move on to the next. It was our turn.

As Fred spun his tale of woe, I said all the same things therapists had been telling him for years. There was nothing wrong with his looks. He was living his life based on a false premise. He had more going for him than he realized. At the same time I was dishing out all this cheery optimism, I couldn't help noticing that by clinging to his invisible, incurable disease, Fred was getting a nice payoff. A small army of professionals had been catering to him for 15 years. He'd been in our town less than 24 hours and we'd already practically given him the key to the city.

I was more than a little suspicious of Fred. I decided we needed to either cure him or expose him as a fraud. There was one problem: when a therapist adopts a cynical attitude about a client, it becomes next to impossible to form a therapeutic relationship. If we were going to work together I needed to keep my suspicions in check and give him the benefit of the doubt.

Over the years Fred had been analyzed, medicated, hypnotized and electro-shocked. He'd painted self-portraits with art therapists, clogged in front of full-length mirrors with dance therapists, sang the blues with music therapists and watched dirty movies with sex therapists. Strangely, he'd never been in group therapy. I decided to plug this hole in his resume.

I was fascinated by group therapy, and I'd taken two classes on it at the university. The theory is simple: human beings are social creatures, and in small groups we tend to replicate our behavior in the larger world. Leaders act like leaders. Wise guys make jokes. Introverts squirm. Nervous Nellies fret. Scapegoats invite abuse. As the group members display their natural tendencies, the therapist helps them develop an awareness of them, and, with the help of the group, address any behavior that seems to be causing them problems. Or something like that.

This seemed like a good approach to use with Fred. For years he'd been listening to what he called "all you counselor types" say he was fine and dandy, and he'd written us off. Shrinks weren't going to admit he was repulsive, he reasoned - they were being paid to make him feel better. But suppose his peers told him the same thing? It seemed worth a shot. I pitched the idea to Anne Blair. She wasn't as enthusiastic as I'd hoped.

"I don't think you can find enough people for a group," she said. "That's why we don't use them here. The substance abusers go to AA and NA, but those are support groups, not therapy groups."

"Fred's problems run a little deeper than AA usually addresses," I pointed out.

"How many people do you need?"

"The ideal group is six or seven, but I can get by with four. I'd need to recruit three more people besides Fred. I can ask the staff for referrals."

"You really want to do this, don't you?"

"I'm really interested in group therapy and Fred seems like a prime candidate. He's counselor-proof, but he might not be peer-proof. If I can only recruit hardcore loonies, I won't do it. He'd just write them off."

"Good luck," she gave me her consent. "I hope it works."

◆ ◆ ◆

I set to work gathering a group. Sifting through a small handful of referrals from my colleagues, I chose three middle-aged women. I thought women might have better luck than men convincing Fred he wasn't an ogre.

Pete gave me Dreama, a thirty-something waitress who was trying work up the courage to leave her philandering lout of a husband. Pete's psychiatric practice centered on psychotropic medications, and Dreama needed counseling. Penelope sent me Sylvia, a 300-pound black woman with a compulsive eating disorder. She was continuing to work with her in movement therapy, but since Sylvia and Fred both had body image issues, I hoped they would find some common ground. Anne Blair referred Cassie, a sensitive soul who was thinking about quitting her job as a bank teller so she could paint full-time.

At our first session the group members shared their competing tales of woe. Fred won. It was Sylvia's turn to give him the standard lecture. "There ain't nothin' wrong with the way you look, Fred," she laid it on him. "You're a fine lookin' man. I'm a whale."

"You can go on a diet," he retorted. "They don't make diets for ugly."

"You're *not* ugly."

"Why should I believe you?"

"Because it's the honest-to-God truth. You think someone's payin' me to try to cheer you up?"

He glanced at me. "Maybe. Maybe this whole thing's a setup."

"Looks aren't everything, Fred," Dreama threw in her two cents. "My husband's got blonde hair, blue eyes and a 9-inch dick, and he's a total asshole."

Cassie blushed. "That's way more information than we need, Dreama."

"Greg said we should say what we think," she defended herself.

"That's the general idea," I agreed. "But I'm not sure we need to know the size of your husband's penis."

Cassie gave her a look of vindication. "I agree. Why should we talk about that?"

162

"You're the one talking about it, Cassie," Dreama came back at her. She returned to the problem at hand. "Fred, how can we convince you that you're not homely?"

"I'm not homely," he said. "I'm grotesque. Homely would be a big improvement."

Sylvia looked at me. "Is there somethin' wrong with this man?"

"That's for the group to decide."

"You're being too hard on yourself, Fred," Cassie gave him a little pep talk. "Different cultures view beauty in different ways. Cultural standards are always changing. Look at the paintings of the Old Masters. Those women in those pictures look overweight by our standards, but soft and round used to be the in thing."

"God bless the Old Masters," Sylvia chimed in.

"Cassie's right, Fred," Dreama agreed. "You shouldn't hold yourself up to some imaginary ideal."

I'd been trying to stay out of it, but I decided to give him a male perspective. "Fred, I'd like to look like Paul Newman or Robert Redford, but obviously I don't. I figure if Helen Keller could deal with being deaf and blind, I can deal with not being a Greek god. Why worry about it? What good is it going to do?"

"There's a difference between not looking like movie star and looking like you escaped from a freak show."

Cassie reached for his hand. "We're trying to help you, Fred."

He snatched it away. "I don't want your damn pity."

"Honey, we're not givin' you pity," Sylvia said. "We're givin' you a swift kick in the butt."

Even Fred laughed.

"Let's not spend the whole session on Fred," I tried to redirect them. "I'm sure the rest of you would appreciate some feedback on your issues, too."

They tried, but they kept coming back to Fred. Time ran out and we agreed to meet the same time next week. I bid them farewell. All in all, things had gone pretty well. Nobody had clammed up or stormed out. I had a feeling this was going to work wonders for these four people.

Anne Blair was a clotheshorse, and she dressed flamboyantly. Occasionally she showed up for work in an outfit that looked more like a costume. When I dropped by her office three days after our first group session, she was wearing a brightly colored top and a necklace of gold doubloons. "You're too early for Cinco de Mayo, Anne Blair," I teased her.

She stood up and modeled it. "Isn't this great? Margo sent it from Acapulco."

"It's fabulous. Not to change the subject, but I'm really pleased with the way our first group therapy session went. Everyone's participating. The women are all fascinated by Fred."

"Cassie's more than fascinated," she gave me some unexpected news. "She took dinner up to him last night and she ended up sleeping with him."

This wasn't something I'd anticipated. "How do we feel about people using the Fellowship Home as a love shack?"

She wasn't judgmental. "They're consenting adults."

"I guess I'm not supposed to know about this, huh?"

"No," she said. "But I thought I'd tell you since you're the Cupid who set them up."

"I didn't set them up! I put them in a therapy group!"

"You gave them the chance to bare their souls," she said. "And they kept baring."

"Now what am I supposed to do?"

"Pretend you don't know about it. I'm a little concerned that Cassie's being drawn into this out of pity. She wants to be Fred's rescuer."

"It'll be interesting to see if Fred's walking with a new spring in his step."

"Keep me posted."

"Don't worry, I will," I promised.

That night I had a call from the hospital emergency room. "We have one of the men from your Fellowship Home here," the nurse informed me. "Can you come get him?"

"There's only one person in our Fellowship Home," I reacted.

"Mr. Frederick Walker?"

"Yes."

"We're releasing him and he needs transportation."

"What did you treat him for?"

"I can't give you that information. You'll have to get it from Mr. Walker."

"Okay, I'll be right there."

I threw on my clothes and hurried to the hospital, suspecting Fred had gone on a bender. The attending physician led me to a cubicle and pulled back the privacy curtain, revealing a man I hardly recognized. Fred had a broken nose, two black eyes, stitches on his right cheek and a missing tooth. I stared at him in amazement. He really was Ugly Fred.

"Dreamath's huthband beat me up," he lisped through swollen lips. "The thavage athhole. The poleeth arrethted him."

"Dreama's husband? Why would Dreama's husband attack you?"

He hung his head.

The doctor picked up his chart. "According to the police, Mr. Walker's attacker found him in bed with his wife."

"FRED! You've slept with two of the women in your therapy group?"

He kept his head down.

I got the picture. "Is this Ugly Fred routine the way you get what you want? Free room and board? Women?" He didn't say anything. "I can't believe this! You're preying on these nice women! I started that group to try to help you!"

"He's ready for discharge," the doctor interrupted my rant. "We don't have any medical reason to keep him."

"Someone else can help him," I said angrily. "He's taken advantage of two very kind-hearted women."

"Thorry," he said. "It won't happen again."

"I have a hard time believing that."

"Please take him with you," the doctor requested. "We don't want to turn him out in the street."

I realized I was overreacting and making a scene. "I'm sorry I'm carrying on like this. I'm a little upset. Come on, Fred, let's go."

We drove back to the home in stony silence. Fred spent the next two days holed up, nursing his wounds. I checked on him and kept him supplied him with Tylenol and Neosporin. On the third day when I went up to the Fellowship Home, Fred and his belongings were gone, only God and Greyhound knew where.

Social workers don't like to talk about their Ugly Freds, but we all have them. When you put your best effort into trying to help someone who's not playing straight with you, a little war goes on in your head between mercy and justice. Should you keep helping someone who's being dishonest? A merciful person would say yes. A just person would say forgiving negative behavior reinforces it and postpones the inevitable lesson they need to learn. You can spend an entire career puzzling over where to draw the line.

Years later I was reading the *Charleston Gazette* and I ran across Fred's obituary. He'd gotten married and he had been living in Charleston. There was no mention of employment, so I guess he'd found a wife who could support him or he'd managed to qualify for disability. I'd like to think his little Lewisburg episode had convinced him it was time to settle down. I'd like to think our efforts weren't wasted, but I'll never know.

Chapter 23
The Alderson Seafood Festival

He was standing by the I-64 entrance ramp holding a sign that said, "Need Ride - Truck Driver." Was he a truck driver who needed a ride or someone who wanted a ride from a truck driver? I didn't usually stop for hitchhikers, but this one had my curiosity. He had on a white button-down shirt and he looked clean cut. *So did Ted Bundy*, I reminded myself as he loped up to the Jeep with a smile on his face.

"I'm trying to get to Ripley," he said through the window.

Ripley was 130 miles away, north of Charleston, and I was only going the first thirty. "I can't help you much," I replied. "I'm only going to the other end of the county."

"That's closer than I am now."

"Okay, come on." He looked like he was in his mid-forties. "Are you a truck driver?"

"I deliver seafood," he explained. "My truck broke down in Virginia. They had to order a part, so I decided to go home instead of sitting in a motel for three days."

"What about the seafood?"

"The company sent another driver to pick it up and cover my route."

We pulled onto the interstate and headed west. "Why did you put truck driver on your sign?"

"So you'd know I'm not just any hitchhiker."

"Must have worked." I held out my hand. "I'm Greg."

"Dooley Trent. If you're ever in Ripley, look me up. I'm the only Trent in the phone book. Hell, I'm probably the only Dooley Trent in the USA. You like to fish, Greg?"

"I grew up in Florida, so I know more about saltwater fishing."

"I've got a stocked pond. You should come by sometime. If you're ever in Ripley, give me a call. I'm serious, man. You're giving me a ride and it's the least I can do."

"Okay, I might," I said, feeling pretty sure that we'd never lay eyes on each other again.

"What line of work are you in, Greg?"

"Social work."

His eyebrows went up. "No kidding? My daughter's a social worker. She went in the Peace Corps."

"Where'd she go to school?"

"WVU."

"So did I. When did she graduate?"

"Two years ago." He pulled out his wallet and showed me a picture of a girl who looked like a Miss America candidate. "Kendra was the first one in our family to go to college," he said proudly. "Do you know her? Kendra Trent?"

"No," I felt sure I would have remembered her. "Where is she stationed in the Peace Corps?"

"Guatemala."

"Didn't they just have an earthquake there?"

"Yeah. She was riding on a bus when it happened."

"Sounds like you've got an adventurous daughter."

"You guys would probably hit it off. She'll be home for Christmas. You ought to come by."

It was the kind of offer fathers didn't usually make – *take my daughter, please*. Was he that desperate to lure her back to the States? I changed the subject. "Where do you make your deliveries?"

"Institutions mostly. I deliver to all the correctional centers in West Virginia." He ticked off a roster of the state's most exclusive gated communities. "Moundsville, Huttonsville, Anthony, Pruntytown, Salem."

"That's an unusual route."

"Everyone tells me that. Think about it. These joints have to serve thousands of people every day. They buy a lot of product. Our company figures it's easier to make a couple of dozen big sales than a couple of hundred little ones. We serve all the prisons in Virginia and West Virginia. It's a good business. Even when the economy's down they've got to feed the inmates."

"Do you go to the federal prison for women in Alderson?"

"Yep, I sure do."

"I live in Alderson. I had a neighbor who was the food service director. Did you know him? Leonard Hall?"

"Hell, yeah. Did he ever tell you about the time the two ladies hid in the back of my truck and tried to escape?"

"No."

"They were helping me unload. When I wasn't looking they slipped into the truck and hid behind some boxes. When I closed the door they went nuts and started pounding on it. They didn't like being locked in a pitch black refrigerator."

"Were they charged with attempted escape?"

"Nah, Leonard cut 'em a break. They were just being stupid. They could have died in the truck."

"That would have been a gruesome discovery."

"So what's a guy your age do for fun in a place like Alderson?"

"I don't know if you'd call it fun, but I'm in the fire department."

"You're a good man," he said. "I can't join the Ripley VFD because I travel. Those guys'll do anything for you. They'll haul their asses out of bed at three o'clock on a winter morning."

"Okay, Dooley, you told me a story so I'll tell you one," I said. "There's a funeral home across from our fire station. The guy who owns it isn't what you'd expect in a funeral director. He's a big practical joker. A while back he bought a new sports car. We got called out on a fire one day and he thought it would be funny to park his car in the station so we couldn't put the truck in after the fire. The only problem was that we back the truck into the station, and it's kind of dark and no one expected a car to be there. We backed the truck into his new car and crushed it."

"That's a good one," he agreed.

"Yeah, you've got to love it when the joke backfires on the joker. This was classic."

We exited the interstate at the Sam Black Church and continued west on Route 60. The broad valley and farms disappeared, and the landscape became more compact. We were on Appalachia's eastern doorstep, where winding roads snaked up hollows and some of the locals worked in the mines. The houses were more modest here than on the other end of the county. Some would say the people were, too.

"Maybe I can help your fire department," Dooley proposed. "Do you guys ever have fundraisers?"

"We talk about it but we never seem to do it."

"Suppose I gave you some seafood."

"What do you mean?"

"Sometimes we've got good stuff we can't sell because the expiration date's coming up, so we have to chuck it. We dump it in the landfill and the seagulls eat it."

"You want to give us expired seafood?"

"It's frozen. You can freeze breaded fish for 6 months. You can freeze shrimp for a year. It's fine. Let's say the expiration date's six weeks from now and we've got more product than orders. We know we'll to have to dump some if it. Suppose I could get it to you before it expires?"

I thought about his offer. I wasn't the world's greatest firefighter. I couldn't sling a 160-pound person over my shoulders and carry them down a 30-foot ladder. But I might be able to help raise the money we needed to buy the Jaws of Life. Seeing the possibilities, I decided to pursue it. "You might have something there, Dooley."

"What would you like? Shrimp?"

"Shrimp would be excellent," I said.

"The next time I'm in Alderson I'll leave some at the prison."

"That would be great. I'll give you my phone number and you can give me a heads up." I figured this was instant karma, my reward for rescuing this man from the side of the road.

"How far did you say you're going?" he asked me.

"Rainelle. It's about fifteen more miles."

"Isn't there a bus station in Rainelle? Maybe I'll take the bus to Charleston and have my wife pick me up there."

"Yeah, there's a Greyhound station."

He pulled out his wallet and counted his money. "Looks like I'm thumbing."

"I can help you out," I offered. "I've got a little cash."

"I can't take your money, man. You might have your own emergency."

"It's no big deal," I assured him. I surveyed the meager contents of my own wallet: $32. Feeling magnanimous, I gave him $25. "Get something to eat. Send me the money when you get home."

He hesitated before he took it. "Are you sure about this?"

"You're doing me a favor, so I'll do one for you. I'll give you my address when I let you out."

"You don't know me from Adam," he said. "I could be conning you."

"Con men don't suggest that they might be conning you. I trust you."

"I owe you for this, man."

"Just remember the seafood. Try to leave us enough for a decent fundraiser."

"I'll leave you plenty," he assured me. "I'll talk to the boss and see if he can throw in a little extra. He can afford it. His family's had the business for sixty years."

"What's the name of your company?"

"Taylor & Sons. It's in Hampton Roads."

By the time we got to Rainelle we were old friends. He printed my address and phone number carefully on a scrap of paper and stuck it in his wallet. "I'll send you the money tomorrow," he promised. "You're a helluva guy, Greg. There aren't many people who'd lend money to a total stranger."

"I don't feel like I'm taking a big risk."

"Good luck with your fire department."

"Thanks." He disappeared in the bus station, and I went on about my business.

I thought about Dooley on my way home that evening. Why had I placed so much faith in this man? I decided it was because his story was too detailed to be something he was inventing on the fly. He hadn't even asked for the money - I'd offered it. He'd seemed hesitant to accept it. Still, when I got home I dialed Directory Assistance and asked for his number in Ripley, just to make sure.

"We don't have a listing for Trent," the operator replied.

Ma Bell's employees often seemed unable to find information that was in plain sight in the phone book, so I wasn't willing to write off the fire department's new benefactor so easily. I thanked her and called Directory Assistance in Hampton Roads and asked for Taylor & Sons. The operator reeled off a list of seafood distributors, but none by this name. I grabbed our local directory and looked up the number of the woman who had replaced Leonard as food service director at the prison after his death.

"I'm really sorry to bother you at home," I apologized, "but I was wondering who delivers your seafood at the prison?"

"Is this a sales call?" she asked.

"No, no - I live here in Alderson. I was Leonard's neighbor. I met a man today who claimed he made seafood deliveries to your prison."

"What kind of seafood?" she sounded puzzled.

"Whatever kind you serve the inmates."

"What makes you think we serve them seafood?"

I hadn't bothered to question Dooley's larger premise - that correctional facilities not only served their inmates seafood, but also served enough of it that a company could turn it into a profitable business. "Do you ever buy seafood?" I grasped at straws.

"Only fish sticks and canned tuna."

"Where do you get it?"

"Sysco."

"Out of Hampton Roads, Virginia?"

"I don't know what you're talking about. Do you think we're serving lobster bisque and shrimp scampi?"

"Crab cakes?" I grasped at straws.

"Do you know the budget I'm working with? Do you think I'd still have my job if I fed these women like they were staying at The Greenbrier?"

"Probably not," I had to admit.

"When we have Lobster Night, I'll give you a call. You can come over and eat with us."

"Thanks," I said. "Sorry to bother you."

I'd been had. Dooley, or whatever his real name was, had asked my occupation and then flashed a picture of his daughter who'd supposedly gone to my school and was in the same line of work. His knowledge of the prison system had probably come from having served time. It was instant karma, all right, my reward for being a complete sap.

My $25 never arrived in the mail, and the Alderson Seafood Festival never took place. But I learned something about con men. They're really, really good at what they do.

Chapter 24
Gloria's Greatest Hit

Every Wednesday our outreach worker, Hazel Kessler, whipped up an elaborate noonday meal in the downstairs kitchen, and the scene in the clinic's basement took on the air of a church supper. Hazel specialized in fried chicken, gravy, homemade rolls, stewed tomatoes and frosted cakes. With tantalizing aromas wafting through the building, most of the staff and many of our clients found their way downstairs. I was fond of this kind of cooking, which reminded me of my southern childhood. I praised the stewed tomatoes so lavishly that Hazel started making them every week.

One week we heard live music drifting up the stairwell with the smells. A woman was singing, and her powerful voice filled the whole building. I followed the sound and found a young woman about my age parked on a stool in the kitchen. She was strumming chords on a beat-up guitar and belting out *One Day at a Time*, a hymn by Kris Kristofferson that had crossed over to the pop charts.

I'm only human, I'm just a woman.
Help me believe
In what I could be and all that I am.
Show me the stairway I have to climb.
Lord for my sake, teach me to take
One day at a time.

One day at a time, sweet Jesus
That's all I'm asking from you.
Just give me the strength
To do everyday what I have to do.
Yesterday's gone, sweet Jesus
And tomorrow may never be mine.
Lord, help me today, show me the way
One day at a time.

"You're really good," I complimented her.

"Thanks," she said shyly. She averted her eyes and I could tell she had some kind of mental impairment. I hadn't noticed her around the clinic before, but Hazel was always gathering up lost souls from the hinterlands and bringing them in for social activities. Her grandmotherly patience allowed her to work with people who progressed at a snail's pace.

Anne Blair appeared in the kitchen. "We could hear you upstairs, dear," she said to our entertainer. "Are you one of Hazel's clients?"

"Yes, ma'am."

"What's your name?"

"Gloria."

"You have a beautiful voice, Gloria. Do you sing professionally?"

"No, ma'am."

"You're very talented."

"Thank you."

I filled my plate at the stove and went into the rec room, where we ate at booths that looked like they belonged in a diner. I dug in enthusiastically and Anne Blair came over with her lunch and sat down. She had a mischievous look in her eyes.

"I've got an idea," she said. "We're having a board of directors meeting next week. I'm going to ask Gloria if she'll come and entertain us. I'll pay her a little something."

"She doesn't seem to mind singing in front of people," I observed.

"Maybe she's a savant," she speculated.

"I've only known one savant," I said. "He was sixteen. He had a bunch of rituals, like opening doors as wide as they would go, but he was a math genius. He was a human computer. You could tell him your birth date and he could instantly tell you the day of the week you were born."

"She might be a musical savant," she said.

"If she is, her talent doesn't extend to instruments," I opined. "She's just strumming basic chords."

"You play the guitar, don't you?"

"I mess around with it some." If you ask a Nashville studio musician if he plays, he'll give you the same line. Guitarists are like coaches; they want to lower your expectations so they can surprise you.

"Why don't you accompany Gloria?" she suggested. "You could pick her up and bring her to the board meeting."

I suspected I was really being asked to deliver the star to her gig, but she was sweetening the pot by making it sound more enticing by asking me to play. Still, it was hard to turn down Anne Blair. "When's the meeting?"

"Monday evening at my house. We're having a social hour before we get started."

"What time?"

"They'll start arriving at five-thirty. I'll gather everyone at six-fifteen and tell them we're having a little entertainment before the meeting. You'll have a chance to meet the board members."

"Sounds good."

Looking pleased with herself she went back to the kitchen and pitched the idea to Gloria, who was sitting on her stool like a lumpy sack of potatoes. She came back in to tell me that Gloria had agreed to perform.

I got our superstar's phone number and told her I'd be in touch. Over the next few days I tried to set up a rehearsal, but nothing seemed to suit her. Monday arrived and we still hadn't practiced or even talked about what she was planning to sing. I arrived at her home early to pick her up, hoping we could have a run-through. Her father answered the door. He had a bushy beard and suspenders; he looked like a white version of Red Foxx.

"I'm sorry for showing up early," I apologized. "I was hoping Gloria and I could practice before we go."

His thick eyebrows went up. "You want to practice here?" he asked, opening the door wider so I could see their tiny dwelling.

"Would it be all right?"

"Son, that girl's got a mighty big set of lungs. When she sings, everything shakes and rattles."

"Can we practice in the yard?"

"You'll freeze out there," her father said. "Gloria doesn't need practice. She's good to go."

"But I do," I protested. "I'm supposed to accompany her."

"You'll be fine," he said. "Don't worry."

I could see that we weren't going to have a rehearsal. Maybe I was being too anal about the whole thing. She was mentally impaired and we were only doing a few songs in an informal setting for a friendly audience. If I messed up no one would notice or care. Plus, with Gloria's standout voice, no one was going to pay attention to the guy playing the guitar. I decided to stop worrying and just wing it.

Gloria appeared in a sequined dress. Apparently she was used to these public appearances. She was the seasoned pro and I was the rank amateur.

"You look nice, Gloria," I said to her.

"Thanks." She got her guitar and we set off on the eight-mile trip to town. My attempts to draw her out were met with one-word replies. I decided to let Gloria be Gloria, and we rode most of the way in silence. Her set list remained a tight-lipped secret.

Anne Blair lived in one of the historic homes on Washington Street, Lewisburg's toniest address. The house had been her parents' home, and she enjoyed letting people know that she was born in it. The rambling old Victorian suited her Grande Dame personality. She loved to entertain, and the house was big enough to accommodate a throng of revelers.

When we walked in I realized I already knew three of the board members – Virginia McLaughlin, the retired warden of the federal prison in Alderson, and two lawyers, Ralph Keightley and Tom Bobbitt. I'd had regular dealings with Ralph, who served as the mental health commissioner and conducted the commitment hearings. If there was anyone who understood our work, it was Ralph. I could see we were going to have a receptive audience. They'd loosened up with cocktails and the room was glowing with good will.

"We have a special treat this evening," Anne Blair announced. "Gloria is going to sing for us. She has such lovely voice. Greg Johnson, who works at the clinic, is going to accompany her on the guitar. Some of you know Greg – he's been with us since May."

Everyone in the room had a drink and a smile. "Okay, Gloria," I cued her. "We're on."

"I need a chair," she said. Someone scrambled to get her one and she squared herself away and launched into her first number. I was relieved to hear her strumming the same song she'd performed at the clinic, which was easy to play. I picked the chords while she sang in her booming contralto. I was sure the neighbors could hear her.

I'm only human, I'm just a woman.
Help me believe
In what I could be and all that I am.
Show me the stairway I have to climb.
Lord for my sake, teach me to take
One day at a time.

One day at a time, sweet Jesus
That's all I'm asking from you.
Just give me the strength
To do everyday what I have to do.
Yesterday's gone, sweet Jesus
And tomorrow may never be mine.
Lord, help me today, show me the way
One day at a time.

Her performance was met by enthusiastic applause. No one in the room was more pleased than Anne Blair. Gloria accepted this attention matter-of-factly. She stood up and bowed, which was probably something she'd seen performers do on TV. She reclaimed her seat and arranged her guitar. Anticipation hung over the room. I sat at the ready, waiting to see what she was going to sing next. She strummed a G chord.

> I'm only human, I'm just a woman.
> Help me believe
> In what I could be and all that I am.
> Show me the stairway I have to climb.
> Lord for my sake, teach me to take
> One day at a time.

> One day at a time, sweet Jesus
> That's all I'm asking from you.
> Just give me the strength
> To do everyday what I have to do.
> Yesterday's gone, sweet Jesus
> And tomorrow may never be mine.
> Lord, help me today, show me the way
> One day at a time.

The applause was slightly less enthusiastic this time around. She stood and took another deep bow.

"Play something else, Gloria," I coaxed her as she settled back on her chair. She hit a G chord again.

> I'm only human, I'm just a woman.
> Help me believe
> In what I could be and all that I am.
> Show me the stairway I have to climb.
> Lord for my sake, teach me to take
> One day at a time.

> One day at a time, sweet Jesus
> That's all I'm asking from you.
> Just give me the strength
> To do everyday what I have to do.
> Yesterday's gone, sweet Jesus
> And tomorrow may never be mine.

Lord, help me today, show me the way
One day at a time.

There was light applause and people were exchanging sidelong glances. Anne Blair hurried forward. "Do you know any other songs, Gloria?" she requested. Gloria shook her head. Anne Blair turned to me in desperation. "Can you play something?"

I wasn't prepared for this request. I didn't have a set list I carried in my wallet in case of musical emergencies. But the board members were studying me expectantly, and anticipation hung in the air. It was suddenly my job to rescue this awkward situation. A song from *The Wizard of Oz* came to mind, one I'd been messing around with a couple of days earlier. I'd figured out my own arrangement of it. It was the only song I could think of at the moment. I started picking and singing.

If I only ...
if I only ...
if I only had a brain.
I could wile away the hours, conferrin' with the flowers
consultin' with the rain.
And my head I'd be scratchin'
while my thoughts were busy hatchin'
if I only had a brain.

I'd unravel every riddle for any indivi'dle
in trouble or in pain.
With the thoughts I'd be thinkin'
I could be another Lincoln
if I only had a brain.

Oh I could tell you why
the ocean's near the shore.
I could think of things I never thunk before
and then I'd sit, and think some more.

I would not be just a nothin'

my head all full of stuffin'
my heart all full of pain.
I would dance and be merry, life would be a ding-a-derry
if I only had a brain.
If I only …
if I only …
if I only had a brain.

I realized too late what I had done. I was following a failed performance by a mentally impaired person with *If I Only Had a Brain*. The only less appropriate song I could have chosen would have been *They're Coming to Take Me Away, Ha-Haaa.* I hoped the generous amount of alcohol the board members had consumed had rendered them tone-deaf to the irony. Ralph, who sometimes played the pipe organ at the Presbyterian Church, was humming *If I Only Had a Brain* as Gloria and I beat a hasty retreat.

We headed back to her home. I praised Gloria for her singing, and she took it in stride. We reached the house and I walked her to the door.

"How'd it go?" her father inquired.

"Fine," I said, without providing any of the grim details.

"I told you so," he said. "You were worrying about nothing."

Curiosity got the better of me. "Does Gloria know any songs besides *One Day at a Time*?" I asked him.

"No, just the one," he said. "But she can really sing it."

Chapter 25
Word Salad

Twyla Barnes had fixed herself up for her appointment at the clinic, but her cockeyed hat and wandering lipstick didn't make the smart impression she probably intended. She looked like a character in a Tennessee Williams play. Twyla hadn't come to the clinic for herself, however. She'd come seeking help for her 25-year-old son, Baxter. "He talks to the TV set," she told me, as she perched on the edge of the chair and clutched her handbag.

"A lot of guys do that," I tried to put her mind at ease. "Especially if they're watching sports."

"Baxter doesn't watch sports. He talks to it when it's not even on. He thinks the people in it are talking to him."

"Oh. How long has he been doing this?"

"Ever since he quit college."

"When was that?"

"Four years ago, when he was in his junior year."

"What do the voices say to him?"

She gave me a funny look. "Why, they don't say anything."

"I mean what does Baxter think they're saying?"

"Why how should I know?"

"Do you ever ask him?"

"I refuse to talk to him when he's acting silly like that."

I could have pointed out that four years of this approach hadn't cured him, but I didn't want to criticize her. "Mrs. Barnes, is there a history of mental illness in your family?"

"Not on *my* side!" She leaned in closer. "Those Barneses are all nuts. Baxter's father committed suicide ten years ago. He turned on the gas and stuck his head in the oven. Baxter found him on the kitchen floor when he came home from school."

"Wow," I reacted. "What a traumatic experience for someone so young."

"I don't believe he's ever gotten over it."

"Does your son have friends?"

"He did when he was in high school. He thinks he's too busy for friends now."

"What's he busy doing?"

She made a disdainful face. "Writing poetry."

"Do his poems make sense?"

"See for yourself." She pulled a folded paper from her bag and gave it to me. "This one took him two weeks."

The poem was called *Socks*, and it consisted of a single sentence:

Socks are little towels for your feet.

I imagined his first collection, *Socks Are Little Towels and Other Insights*, by Baxter Barnes. Very interesting." On one level the little poem was very clever. I knew I would remember it word-for-word for the rest of my life, which is more than I can say for most poetry.

"He had socks strewn all over the apartment," she filled in the picture. "He wouldn't let me touch them. He studied them like they were Holy Scripture."

"Does Baxter have a job?"

"He thinks writing this gibberish is his job. He keeps his poems in a folder he calls 'the body of my work'."

"Has he ever held a job?"

"What kind of work could a boy like that find? This morning he told the mailman I was an alien who'd taken his mother's place! I asked him what in the world had given him that idea and he said he could read my mind."

She was describing classic psychotic symptoms: voices, delusions, paranoia, social isolation, a feeling of special powers. My hunch was that we were dealing with schizophrenia. Schizophrenia usually manifests in the late teens or early twenties, and from what she said it sounded like Baxter's symptoms had started appearing around age twenty. I didn't want to alarm her with a scary-sounding word like schizophrenia, so I soft-pedaled it. "Mrs. Barnes, we need to see Baxter right away. He might need to be on medication. He might even need to be hospitalized so they can figure out the best kind for him."

"You'll never get that boy to go to a hospital. I couldn't even get him to come with me today."

"Would you mind if I made a home visit? Where do you live?"

She looked embarrassed. "Almost Heaven."

The Almost Heaven apartment complex was owned by a landlord who thought he was doing people a favor to rent them his roach-infested dwellings. The tiny units were filled with the kind of downtrodden souls who received holiday bags of food and toys from service organizations. Twyla knew she deserved better, but the life insurance policy Duke Barnes had purchased before he'd taken his life had contained a suicide clause he hadn't bothered to read.

She answered the door looking less put-together than she had at the clinic. Her mousy gray hair was poking up like a meringue. "It's Mr. Johnson from that mental health place," she announced before I could make a less threatening introduction.

I'd pictured a starving young artist – a serious guy in a black turtleneck and horn-rimmed glasses - but Baxter was a moonfaced, well-fed artist. He had an impish smile, like he was party to some cosmic joke the rest of us didn't get. My visit caught him off-guard. "Mother, who is this person?" he demanded to know. "Is this another one of your ill-conceived plans to ruin my life?"

"If you'd just act like a normal person, Baxter ..."

"Isn't it obvious that I don't want to be a normal person?"

She turned to me pleadingly. "He doesn't want to be a normal person."

"Your mother showed me your poem about socks, Baxter. You're right – they are little towels for your feet. You captured the essence of socks in seven words."

"Let this man in, Mother," he changed his tune. "Don't leave him standing out there like a Jehovah's Witness."

"Maybe he doesn't want to come in, Baxter. We live in a trash heap."

"When I win the Pulitzer Prize, I'll buy us a new home," he offered grandly.

"You're not Ernest Hemingway, Baxter."

"Mother, please don't compare me to that alcoholic egomaniac."

Twyla opened the door wider and I got my first good look at their cramped apartment. Belongings were piled in every nook and cranny; it looked more like a storage unit than a place where people lived. Blankets and a pillow behind the couch suggested the kitchen/dining/living area also served as Baxter's bedroom. Twyla's bedroom door was open and there was barely room for the bed. In an odd touch, the walls in the apartment were painted bright yellow. It seemed like a desperate effort to cheer up their gloomy quarters.

Twyla saw me staring at the walls. "The yellow was Baxter's idea."

"It's the color of creativity," he explained. "It helps my writing."

I took a seat at the kitchen table. "I'm curious about your writing, Baxter. What inspired you to write about socks?"

He thought about it, and he seemed to enter another realm. "Shoes and socks dripped on the floor working against each other," he explained.

"You're not making any sense, Baxter," Twyla said. "The man asked you a simple question."

"It's called word salad," I let her know. The technical term was schizophasia, a jumble of meaningless words symptomatic of schizophrenia.

"Word salad," Baxter repeated. "I'm a word chef."

"A lot of famous writers have made word salad," I pointed out. "John Lennon's song *I Am the Walrus* is word salad. So is Lewis Carroll's poem *Jabberwocky*. Some writers enjoy playing around with words, even when they don't mean anything."

He studied me curiously. "Are you an English teacher?"

"No, I'm a social worker, but I like to read. I was fascinated by *Socks*. Will you show me more of your poetry?"

He went over to a swayback bookcase and retrieved a folder, presumably "the body of his work". He shuffled through the pages and pulled out a poem called *Flames*.

Joker flames playing handy poker.

Socks had a clarity this effort seemed to lack. "Interesting," I commented, handing it back to him.

"Try this one," he gave me *Dancing*.

Heavy dancing flying buttresses pickled pink.

"That's a unique combination of words."

"Please don't encourage him with this nonsense," Twyla requested. "He needs a job. He needs to earn his own money. He needs to take care of himself so I won't have to support him the rest of his life."

"I need a vacation," Baxter offered his own opinion.

"A vacation!" she exclaimed. "Your whole life is a vacation!"

He gave me a poem called *Sleep*. "Read this one."

Sleep is looking at the insides of your eyelids.

"I like this one," I said. "It's more like *Socks*." Apparently when it came to writing, he had his good days and his bad days. "Your mother says voices in the television talk to you. What do they say?"

"My muse is inside the TV," he explained. "His name is Cedric. He's from England."

"There's no one in the TV, Baxter!" Twyla yelled at him. "It's all in your head!"

I added a schizophrenic named Baxter with a muse named Cedric to my case list.

The following week Baxter agreed to hospitalization after I convinced him that his stay was going to be like a mini-vacation. I drove him over to Appalachian Regional Hospital in Beckley, about an hour away. As we talked, one minute he'd make perfect sense and the next minute he'd be confused and delusional. Some schizophrenics come and go like a fiddler's elbow, and Baxter was one of them. He had a good sense of humor, but his jokes and stories usually fell apart before he reached the end. He did manage to keep it together long enough pull a little stunt on me at the hospital.

We'd taken an elevator to the second floor and they'd buzzed us into the psych ward. As we approached the nurses' station Baxter gave the nurse a smile. "Hello!" he said officiously. "I'm Greg Johnson from the mental health clinic." He pointed to me. "And this is the patient, Baxter Barnes."

The nurse turned to me. "Hello, Baxter," she said in a reassuring voice. "It's nice to have you here."

"Very funny, Baxter," I said. I turned back to the nurse with the real explanation. "I'm Greg Johnson. He's Baxter Barnes."

She looked back and forth at us, and I realized she didn't know who was telling the truth.

Baxter wheeled and started up the hallway. "Keep us posted on his progress," he called over his shoulder.

"I really am Greg Johnson," I tried to convince her. I pulled out my wallet and showed her my driver's license.

"Who's your administrator?" she quizzed me.

"Anne Blair Alderson."

"Hold your horses, Baxter," she called to her departing patient. "You're not going anywhere. This is a locked ward."

Baxter faced his captor with resignation. "I'm inspecting the undercover scenario like a hot otter," he explained helpfully.

"Now I'm *sure* which one of you is Baxter."

"I have a little present for you before I go," I let him know. I pulled a poem from my shirt pocket. "I wrote this for you." I read it to him.

"Baxter, the poet in a bright yellow room,
writes chronicles of his time,
tossing word salads and serving them up
without any reason or rhyme.
He thinks and composes, studies, discloses
on subjects both weighty and small,
revealing their essence with bright luminescence,
holding his readers in thrall.
Some day, some way, when all is clear
the world will boast, 'Baxter was here.' "

He stared at me in wonderment. "Are you giving this to me?"
"Sure, it's gift."
It was pure doggerel, but from the look on his face, I knew I couldn't have made him any happier if I'd given him a thousand bucks. I could see we were going to be friends.

Chapter 26
The Preacher's Kids

The man in the waiting room was wearing a black suit and a black hat with a flat brim. His plain clothing and beard made him look Amish, but he had a mustache and Amish men didn't usually have mustaches. Our appointment calendar identified him only as James Smith. I stuck out a hand. "James? I'm Greg Johnson."

We shook hands and he kept his head bowed. I thought I was dealing with someone who was very shy. As soon as we reached my upstairs office he took off his hat and sunglasses. Then, bizarrely, he removed his fake beard. "Do you know me now?"

I studied his jowly countenance. He looked a little like Richard Nixon, but it seemed unlikely that the disgraced former president was seeking our services. "I'm sorry, I don't," I admitted.

"I'm Pastor Eddie Dean Dillon," he said. "You've probably seen my show on Channel 6."

"Actually, I don't think I have."

He tucked the beard in his hat and placed it on the desk, where it nested like a sleeping squirrel. "I don't want anyone to know I'm here," he said emphatically, helping himself to a chair. "I'm sorry I didn't speak to you down there, but people recognize my voice from *The Hour of Revelation*. The show's made me a public figure. I pastor a church in Summers County and I conduct tent revivals, too."

"You sound like a busy man."

"I serve the Lord with gladness."

"Do you live in Summers County?"

"Yes, we live on Route 20, between Hinton and Pipestem."

"You have two mental health centers closer to you," I pointed out. "FMRS in Hinton and Southern Highlands in Princeton."

"People are going to recognize me in those places," he insisted. "I can't have that. The flock doesn't expect to see their shepherd in a mental health center." He clasped his hands and rested them on my desk. "I'm here about my children."

He told me about his son and daughter, twin 16-year-olds who were going through a rough patch. "Last night Zeb put my car in the Greenbrier River. He was supposed to be working on a school project at a friend's house, but he was out drinking. On the way home he missed a turn. He went over a small embankment and drove into the river. He swam to the other side and spent the night at a friend's house so he wouldn't get arrested for DUI. You can imagine our surprise when the phone rang at three in the morning and the police told us our car was sitting in four feet of water! I had to have it towed. I'm driving a rental."

"Wow. You must be really frustrated."

"I've reached the end of my rope with that boy. Enough is enough. I've got to do something."

"Have there been other incidents?"

"Would you call sideswiping three parked cars an incident?"

"Yes, especially if mine was one of them. Was alcohol involved?"

"Alcohol," he said disdainfully, "is always involved. And then there was the time he streaked one of my revivals, waving a can of Budweiser."

"That sounds more like a prank."

"A prank to totally humiliate his father!"

"That's quite a litany of sins for a 16-year-old. I'm surprised you're still letting him drive."

"We restrict his driving to school-related activities. So of course he tells us everything is related to school."

"It sounds like Zeb's spinning out of control."

"Out of control!" he exclaimed, jowls aquiver. "Out of control doesn't begin to describe what that boy's put us through!"

"You say your daughter's giving you problems, too?"

His sigh sounded like the song of the humpback whale. "Delilah thinks she's in love with a 30-year-old mechanic. She's threatening to elope if we try to stop her from seeing him. At least if she runs off, we won't have to see her riding around on the back of his motorcycle, clinging to him like a monkey. I don't know how we managed to raise two juvenile delinquents. They grew up in a God-fearing home."

"They haven't necessary rejected those values," I said. "They're just teenagers."

"The Lord has always given me guidance, but He doesn't seem to be helping me much with this one. Our children are bringing shame on our family. They're making a mockery of my ministry." He leaned forward. "Will you have a word of prayer with me, brother?"

"That's not what we do here. If that's the kind of help you're looking for, there's a pastoral counseling center in Charleston."

"I'm not going to a pastoral counseling center! I'm not telling another clergyman about this! It's embarrassing enough to have to come here."

"Okay, fair enough. We'll talk about your family dynamics and I'll want to meet with your wife and your children."

"My wife doesn't need to be involved in this."

"Is there a reason she can't participate?"

"There's no point in both of us coming here. If you've got suggestions, I'll pass them along to her."

This seemed like an odd arrangement considering the family nature of the problem. I played a hunch. "Do you and your wife ever disagree about how to handle your kids?"

"We have our differences of opinion."

"How do you resolve them?"

"Paula accepts my authority as head of the family."

"So you always win?"

"Winning has nothing to do with it," he insisted. "Ephesians Chapter 5 instructs wives to be submissive to their husbands."

I imagined the feminists in my class at the university wailing and gnashing their teeth. But we weren't talking about theology, so I stuck to the basics. "I'm just trying to understand how your family works,

Eddie. When young people act out, it's important to look at the larger picture. We need to figure out what they're rebelling against."

"I think that's pretty obvious. They're rebelling against everything."

"Any idea why?"

"You'll have to ask them."

Eddie had identified his children as the problem and he wanted me to fix them. It hadn't seemed to dawn on him that he might need some tinkering under the hood himself.

On Sunday morning I tuned in to *The Hour of Revelation* out of curiosity. Eddie was pacing the sanctuary of his little church, thundering like a confident prophet, assuring his viewers they would receive countless blessings if they supported his ministry. I had grown up Catholic and I didn't really understand this kind of religion, but Eddie probably didn't have much use for the papacy or the liturgy either. Instead of a choir and a pipe organ, he had Brother Bob and Sister Hallie playing boom-chuck rhythms on a guitar and tambourine. The *Hour's* production values were minimal, with a stationary camera peering over the heads of the faithful from the back of the church. I guessed Eddie was either footing the bill for the broadcast himself or taking advantage of some FCC mandate requiring stations to carry so many hours of local programming.

The highlight of the service came when he summoned a red-haired, freckle-faced boy named Franklin, who looked like he'd stepped out of a Norman Rockwell painting, to join him in the sanctuary. He gave him a little pop quiz.

"Now, Franklin, we all know you're a good student. Isn't that right?"

"I reckon," Franklin said with an aw-shucks grin.

"Well, son, tell us what they taught you in school about fire safety. What are you supposed to do if your clothes catch on fire?"

"Stop, drop and roll?" the boy asked tentatively.

Eddie threw up his arms like his young assistant had scored the winning touchdown in the Super Bowl. "That's right! Stop, drop and roll! Now, Franklin, I want you to give us a little demonstration. Show us what you'd do if your clothes were on fire."

"Right here?" the boy asked.

"Yes! Right here! Right now! Suppose your pants caught fire. What would you do?"

The boy threw himself on the carpet and flopped around energetically. The congregants craned their necks for a better view of the action. You had to give Eddie points for showmanship. There probably weren't many channel surfers switching to other stations. Franklin hopped up and Eddie gave him a pat on the back and sent him back to his pew. He turned his attention to his flock. "Friends, I've got bad news for you today," he said with a long face. "Stop, drop and roll won't work in hell!"

He described people writhing in flames and roasting on coals in the netherworld. It was classic fire-and-brimstone, meant to scare the beejezus out of his congregation and home viewers. I'd had enough. I turned off the TV and tried to imagine what it would be like to grow as Pastor Eddie Dean Dillon's son or daughter.

I was sitting with Zeb and Delilah Dillon at a picnic table overlooking Sandstone Falls, on the New River. I thought meeting in this park would be less threatening for them than coming to the clinic. I'd gotten them out of class and we pretty much had the place to ourselves; the only other visitors were in the river, fishing in hip boots and shooting the rapids in inflatable kayaks.

The Dillon twins were fraternal, which seems like the wrong word to describe a boy and a girl. They were trying not to give any clues that they were preacher's kids. Zeb's long brown hair was tied back in a ponytail. Delilah's was bleached blonde, and she'd been a little heavy-handed in the makeup department. I expected their father to be the main topic and they didn't disappoint me.

"He's a total phony," Zeb complained bitterly. "He tells people they're going to hell if they use alcohol. Meanwhile he's sneaking around buying it himself."

"What?"

"He collects limited edition liquor bottles," Delilah elaborated. "He goes shopping where people don't know him, down in the Carolinas."

"What kind of alcohol are we talking about?"

"You name it," Zeb said. "If it looks like Elvis or the Washington Monument or a turkey, he buys it. He even buys weird shit like rye whiskey. Our whole basement's full of bottles. We're not supposed to say anything to anybody about it."

This was an unexpected twist. "Collecting limited edition liquor bottles seems like an unusual hobby for an evangelist. Does he drink it?"

They both shook their heads. "He says they're not worth anything if they've been opened," Delilah explained.

"How do you know he doesn't drink it?" I pressed them, still trying to make sense of all this.

Zeb grinned. "Because me and my friends do. We steam the seals off and fill the bottles with water and glue the seals back on. He's got a water collection and he doesn't know it."

The irony in this situation was as multi-layered as a baklava. Eddie was preaching against the evils of drink while he was enthusiastically supporting the liquor industry. He was upset about his son's partying ways, but he was unknowingly enabling them. And, in a reverse Miracle at Cana, his spirits had turned to water. I hardly knew where to start. "Tell me about your mother," I invited them.

"Mom's okay," Zeb weighed in. "You can reason with her. But she does what Dad tells her. He says God created Adam before Eve because men are supposed to be in charge and women are supposed to be their helpers."

"*Helpmates*," Delilah corrected him.

"Do you see your father as the main problem?"

"He's the *only* problem," Zeb replied. "I hate the way he stands up in front of people and acts like he knows everything. He doesn't know shit."

"Speaking of shit, you've been giving your folks a lot of it lately, Zeb. Partying when you're supposed to be doing schoolwork, driving under the influence, leaving the scene of an accident. If you're lucky you'll only end up with broken limbs. If you're not, you'll end up in a body bag."

"Man, now you sound like a preacher," he accused me. It was probably the worst insult he could think of.

"I'm just telling you what I've seen. The party always comes to an end." I turned to Delilah. "And you're dating a guy who's nearly old enough to be your father. That probably isn't the best idea in the world."

"Jason's cool," she said defensively.

"If you guys are looking for ways to get back at your father, you've found some good ones. I just hope you don't end up ruining your own lives while you're trying to prove something."

Zeb eyed me suspiciously. "Did Dad pay you to give us this lecture?"

"Nope. I'm sure it's hard being a preacher's kid. But things are never going to get better at home if you won't come halfway."

"He won't come the other half," Delilah complained. "He thinks God's on his side."

"I'm pretty sure God's neutral. Are you interested in trying to patch things up with your folks? Would you like your lives to get back to normal?"

"Our lives were never normal," Zeb said.

I had a sinking feeling he was telling the truth.

The night before Eddie was scheduled to return to the clinic I couldn't sleep. He was a difficult man, but I needed to find a way we could work together. After a lot of tossing and turning I came up with a conversation starter.

As I'd hoped, he showed up in the same disguise he was wearing before. "You know, Eddie, the first time I saw you in that outfit I thought you were Amish," I told him.

"I suppose I do," he conceded. "I found this hat in a yard sale. The beard came from a shepherd's costume we use in our Nativity pageants."

"We studied the Amish in sociology," I said. "It's a hard sect to peg. We tend to think of them as ultra-conservative, but in Europe they were considered radical troublemakers."

"We don't have any Amish people in West Virginia," Eddie reacted. "They're in Virginia and Ohio and Pennsylvania, but for some reason they never got established here."

"In a lot of ways they're admirable," I stayed with the topic. "They place a high value on family and community."

"They live by their faith," he agreed.

"When it comes to teenagers they do something most of us would view as extreme. Have you ever heard of rumspringa?"

"About what?"

"Rumspringa. It means *running around* in old German. The Amish consider the teenage years a time for experimentation and rebellion, and they just let it happen. They call it rumspringa."

"What do you mean they just let it happen?"

"They let their sons and daughters sample what the world has to offer. They have to decide if they want to leave their community or get baptized into it. Rumspringa lasts anywhere from a couple of months to a couple of years, whatever it takes. If they want to dress in regular clothes and drive cars and go to dances, their parents don't interfere."

"That's hardly rebellious compared to what my children are doing."

"Yes, but the Amish overlook the harder stuff, too – the sex and alcohol and drugs. They tolerate things they'd never tolerate otherwise. They view it as part of adolescence."

"You can't mean they just let them do - whatever?" he asked incredulously.

"I know it's hard to believe, but it's true. I was surprised when I heard about it."

"That's the most ridiculous thing I've ever heard."

"It is risky," I had to agree. "But 90% of the kids return to their community and ask to be baptized. Do other religions have that kind of retention rate? Giving them so much freedom seems to take the wind out of their sails. All the forbidden fruit seems exciting, but then they discover it's not very satisfying. The Amish are actually growing in numbers while other churches are shrinking."

"If my members had six or seven children our numbers would be growing, too," he said defensively. "What's your point? Why are you telling me this?"

"Because I think Zeb and Delilah are having a rumspringa."

"They're not doing it with my permission."

"That makes it even more exciting. Did you go through a rebellious period when you were young?"

"I didn't have anything to rebel against. My parents were terrible examples. My father was a drunk and we had a hard time financially. My mother was arrested twice for shoplifting."

"So you rebelled by embracing religion?"

"If I'd followed their examples I'd be in jail! My father took me to a prostitute on my sixteenth birthday! It was the most embarrassing moment of my life. That's the kind of judgment he had. I've never told my children about it."

"So you've tried to live by higher standards?"

"And now Zeb and Delilah are turning out like my parents! I don't know how to stop it. I'm used to getting respect from people, but my own children don't respect me at all."

"When you grow up with a parent who makes his living telling people to walk the straight and narrow, it's not hard to figure out how to rebel," I pointed out what was probably obvious to everyone but him. "It's so common in preachers' kids there's even a name for it – P.K. Syndrome."

"I don't care if there's a name. Is there a cure?"

"Most young people grow out of it. Time is on your side."

"Time! I don't have time to wait for this nonsense."

"There is something you can do in the meanwhile, but it's pretty radical."

He leaned forward with interest. "What?"

"Talk less and listen more. Try to figure out how they view things."

This wasn't what he wanted to hear. "You don't want me to exercise my duty to give them parental guidance?" he accused me.

"Only if you can do it without it coming off as criticism."

"I thought you were going to have some sort of sensible suggestion."

"Sending Zeb off to a treatment program or putting Delilah in boarding school may be like the kind of suggestion you're looking for, but that won't solve your problem. They'd just be more resentful in the long run. My initial impression is that they're fairly normal kids with an unusual family situation."

"What's so unusual about my family?"

"They have an evangelist father with a liquor bottle collection."

This hit him like a Mack truck. "What does my hobby have to do with this?"

"It's a symbol to Zeb and Delilah that you don't practice what you preach."

"What are you talking about?"

"Teenagers have a radar for adult inconsistency. Whenever they catch us saying one thing and doing another, they interpret it to mean that we're phonies, which reinforces the idea that they don't have to listen to us about anything."

"A limited edition liquor bottle collection means I'm a *phony?*" he asked. "I'm doing it to help fund their college!"

"They can't reconcile your opposition to alcohol with your support of the industry."

"I've never touched a drop of that liquor."

I wanted to say, "Yes, but your son sure has," but I couldn't break Zeb's confidence. "Don't you think it's a temptation keeping all that liquor in your basement? Especially when you know Zeb's attracted to alcohol?"

"Those bottles are sealed," he huffed.

"How big is your collection?"

"I probably have three or four hundred bottles. Most of them are in mint condition. Some of the Jim Beams and miniatures are very valuable. I have a Dom Pérignon worth $250."

It seemed easier for him to talk about his bottle collection than about his children. By the time Eddie left the clinic he had plenty to think about. He was so distracted, he started to leave without his disguise and I had to remind him to put it on.

Eddie took our conversation far more seriously than I thought. The next time we met I planned to talk about with him about substance abuse counseling for Zeb, but he had a surprise announcement. "I sold my bottle collection," he told me. "You were right. It didn't make sense with my ministry. I sold them to a collector in Tennessee."

"That's great, Eddie," I congratulated him.

"Twenty-seven thousand dollars," he said proudly.

I chewed on my lip and thought about the poor soul who'd forked over twenty-seven grand for Pastor Eddie Dean Dillon's bottles of water. *The Hour of Revelation* was yet to come.

Chapter 27
Somebody There

"I used to be a barber, you know."

The mottled hands of the 82-year-old gentleman in my office were shaking slightly, so it was a bit of a stretch to picture him standing behind a barber's chair, cutting hair. "Where did you work, Mr. Addison?"

"Archie's Barber Shop in Darley Dale."

"Was that in England?" Archibald Addison had already told me he was from Great Britain, which I could have guessed from his distinctive accent and the fact that he was wearing a tweed coat over a wool sweater, the kind of spring uniform older Brits seemed to favor.

"Aye, lad, 150 miles north of London. Darley's a fine place, heaven on earth."

Archie's daughter Stella had brought him to the clinic, complaining that her father was turning increasingly grouchy. She wanted us to prescribe a mood elevator to lift his spirits. I was serving as the intake worker that day, so it was my job to interview Archie, write up his history and make an educated guess about what he needed.

"You could use a haircut," he noticed one of my needs before I got to his. "You should have it tapered on the sides so it doesn't cover your ears."

"My hair's naturally bushy on the sides," I told him. "If I had it cut today, two days from now it would be over my ears again."

"You need the sides thinned. A good barber could take care of that."

"I appreciate your professional opinion, Archie. When did you give up barbering?"

"When they moved me here two years ago. I was working part-time before I came."

"When who moved you here?"

"My daughter and son-in-law. They mean well I suppose, but I shouldn't have let them do it."

"Tell me about yourself," I invited him. "Let's talk about your life back in England, and then we'll work up to your move to the States."

He told me about his service in World War II, when he was based on Salisbury Plain and took part in D-Day, his marriage to his childhood sweetheart, their two children and three grandchildren, and his wife's death from cancer. With the exception of his Army service and his recent move to the States, his entire life had been played out in Darley Dale, a town in Derbyshire that was about the size of Lewisburg. I gathered that his barbershop had been a local hangout and he'd been a popular man.

"Stella and Michael expect me to spend all my time watching the telly," he complained. "I don't fancy that."

"So you were happier in Darley Dale?"

He looked me in the eyes and said with conviction, "I'm a bloody nobody here, lad. I'm somebody there."

Stella seemed surprised that instead of sending her father to our psychiatrist for medication, I wanted to talk with her. She and her brother Geoffrey, who still lived in Darley Dale, had decided it was her turn to care for their aging father. Stella and Michael's own children were grown and gone, and they'd created an apartment for Archie in their home. They both worked at The Greenbrier, where she was a housekeeper and he was a doorman. Their work schedules meant that Archie was spending a lot of time by himself at home.

"We know Dad doesn't like it here," she conceded after I'd told her what he'd said. "We've tried to get him involved in activities at the senior center, but he won't have any part of it. He's stubborn."

"Does he have friends here?"

"He's not interested in making new friends. The neighbors say hello and the people who come over are nice to him, but he doesn't have any friends of his own."

"I guess he doesn't want to hang out at Flanagan's Barber Shop?"

"I suggested that," she told me. "He said he didn't fancy listening to blokes he doesn't know talking about other blokes he doesn't know. Even if he did, I don't think Mr. Flanagan wants to provide day care for the elderly."

"What about sending him back to Darley Dale?"

She hesitated, and I could tell she'd given it some thought. "That wouldn't be very fair to my brother and his wife, now would it? It would look like we don't want any responsibility for Dad."

"Is there a reason your father can't go back and live on his own?"

"He's getting on in years. He's feeble. He's never fixed his own meals or washed up the dishes. Mum took care of him until she died, and Geoff and Clara took care of him after that. Now its our turn."

"How would Geoff react if you told him things weren't working out?"

"He'd think it was my fault that he's not settling in. You know how siblings are."

"Does Archie have an income? Are you responsible for him financially?"

"He gets his Old Age Pension, but it's a pittance. We support him."

"What if you offered to contribute to his care if he moved back in with Geoff and Clara?"

Clearly this wasn't the conversation she was expecting to have. "Can't you just fix him up with some medicine?" she begged me.

"Stella, we could mask his symptoms with pills, but they aren't going to solve his problem. There's only one cure for homesickness."

"Even if Geoff and Clara would take him in, we can't manage to send him. It took us months to save up enough to bring him here. Geoff doesn't have much money either. He's a clerk and Clara works in a laundry."

"I certainly understand that. I don't have the money to go to Europe either. But suppose you could afford to send him back home. Would you consider talking with Geoff and Clara about it?"

"Maybe."

"The clinic is a nonprofit corporation," I told her. "Sometimes people make charitable gifts. We might be able to buy Archie a plane ticket. I'm not promising anything, but why don't you talk with Geoff?"

Stella and her brother agreed that their father belonged in Darley Dale, and they worked out a financial arrangement. Now all we had to do was find a way to send Archie home. I started to talk with Anne Blair, whose first impulse would have been to buy the ticket herself. Then I had a better idea: I decided to consult with Margo, our globetrotting psychologist. If anyone at the clinic had expertise on air travel it was Margo. Fortunately she was in town and I caught her after she'd finished administering a Rorschach inkblot test.

She seemed intrigued when I told her about Archie. "That's a very interesting case," she reacted. The fact that it involved international travel clearly captured her attention. "Are you thinking about Heathrow or Gatwick?"

"What do you mean?"

"London has two major airports," she educated me. "We need to use the one closest to his home."

"Whichever one has the cheapest flight. Beggars can't be choosers."

"I'll ask my travel agent to donate the ticket," she shrugged off the cost. "God knows I give him enough business. Where is your client going?"

"Darley Dale. It's 150 miles north of London."

"Then you'll want Heathrow. Gatwick's on the south side. When does he want to go?"

"Yesterday. He's 82 and he's not getting any younger."

"I'll see what I can do," she said. "Does he need transportation to Darley Dale?"

"I imagine his son can pick him up the airport."

She looked disappointed. I think she wanted the challenge of wangling a free train ride and an overnight stay in a five-star hotel, too. If she couldn't make the trip herself, she wanted to live vicariously.

Margo managed to get Archie a complimentary ticket, and he was scheduled to leave on Thursday. Stella called me on Tuesday and said that her dad wanted to see me. I had a sinking feeling that after all this effort on his behalf, he'd changed his mind about repatriation. Unpredictable clients were always throwing us curve balls. You'd go to the trouble to arrange something, and then they'd decide they didn't want it. I hated this aspect of social work, but I was getting used to it. "Do you know why he wants to see me?" I asked her.

She wouldn't shed any light on it. "The two of you need to discuss it," is all she said.

That afternoon I met him in the waiting room and helped him climb the stairs to my second floor office. He was carrying a Dopp kit, and I thought it probably contained medication or something else he needed. I pulled a chair up to the desk for him, but he remained standing. "I want to give you something," he said. "I want to give you a haircut." He opened his leather pouch slowly and pulled out electric clippers, scissors, thinning shears and a barber cape.

I laughed. "You really think I need a haircut that badly, Archie?"

"This is how I'm thanking you for helping me," he explained. "Sit down." He pointed at the chair I had pulled out for him.

He put the cape around me and went to work, going through the same motions he'd gone through countless times in his barbershop. He clipped and trimmed and thinned and combed, stepping back occasionally to inspect his work. His hands were trembling a bit, but he worked confidently until he reached what he decided was the finished product. "There," he said. "Have a look."

Since the clinic had been a girls' dormitory in its previous life, our offices were equipped with sinks and mirrors. I stepped up to the mirror to check out my haircut. The parts that usually fluffed out on the sides were behaving themselves. I turned back to him. "It's taken me years to find a good barber and you're leaving the country."

"Do you fancy it?"

"Yes, I really do."

"Do you know the difference between a bad haircut and a good haircut?" he asked me.

"No, what?"

"Three days," he said. He chuckled at his own joke.

"This is exactly what I needed, Archie."

Looking pleased with himself the retired barber gathered up the tools of his trade and placed them carefully them back in his Dopp kit.

"Archie, do you remember when you told me were a nobody here but you were somebody in Darley Dale?"

"I do."

"I disagree. You're somebody here, too."

He said goodbye and left the office smiling contentedly. I had the feeling he probably smiled all the way back to Darley Dale.

Chapter 28
Two Weddings and a Turkey

I looked at the wedding invitation I'd been handed by the beaming young man in my office, printed on a copy machine and clipped out with scissors. Medwin Bales and Lucy Taggert were getting married the next day in an outdoor ceremony at his mother's home. I could see from his eager expression that he was counting on my being there.

Medwin considered me his friend, even though my role in his life had been ancillary. I'd done two favors for his counselor at Vocational Rehabilitation, Jack McManus. I'd talked him out of running off with the carnival at the State Fair, and I'd delivered him to a janitorial training program in the Charleston area when Jack was hospitalized after a heart attack. Medwin and Lucy had met their first day at the training program. They were both slow learners with borderline intelligence. In some ways this meant they were a match made in heaven, but in other ways it meant they had a rough road ahead.

"I'll be there, Medwin," I promised him. "May I bring my fiancée?"

"Sure," he said. "You need to bring the cake, too."

"The cake?"

"Gwen's making it. We need someone to bring it."

Gwen Clingman served home cooked meals in the back of her small market on Washington Street, and she did catering and cakes on the side. Gwen was a tiny woman with a big heart, and I had a feeling Medwin and Lucy were getting a deep discount on the cake, if they were paying her anything. "What time should we pick it up?"

"Two o'clock. The wedding's at three."

"Then we'd better pick it up at one-thirty, just to make sure. We might get there a little early, but I can help set up chairs or something."

He gave me a puzzled look. "What chairs?"

"You don't have any chairs?"

He shook his head.

"How many people are coming?"

He shrugged.

"How many are you inviting?"

He held up his little stack of invitations, which he was apparently delivering in person around town.

"Did your mother send out invitations?"

"No. She said I had to do it."

"What about Lucy's family?"

"They're not invited," he said. "She doesn't like them."

"Have you gotten your marriage license?"

His brow furrowed. "What's that?"

"It's a legal document that gives you permission to get married in West Virginia. You need to go to the courthouse with Lucy and apply for it. Take along photo ID's and if you have your birth certificates take them with you."

"I won't have time to give out the invitations," he complained.

"You've *got* to do this, Medwin. If you don't have a marriage license, you can't get married." I reached in my wallet and gave him a twenty. "This is a wedding present. Use it to buy your license. If they tell you there's a waiting period let me know. I can call the judge and try to get it waived."

"Thanks." He took the money and he dashed off.

"Oh my God," Libby reacted as she looked at the elaborately decorated three-tiered cake, balanced on miniature Doric columns.

"There's no way we can take this in the Jeep. It won't make it to the next block."

"I'll take it apart," Gwen offered. "You can put it back together when you get there."

I was surprised by the cake's size. "I don't think Medwin realizes how many people this cake will feed," I said to Gwen.

"He said they're expecting two or three hundred," Gwen reported.

"I think his count is off. It's probably going to be more like 20 or 30. He just started inviting people yesterday."

"Do you want me to separate it into three cakes?" she asked.

"Yes, please," Libby requested. "If we're late, they'll just have to wait for their cake." She went to work and helped Gwen disassemble her culinary masterpiece. They lifted the tiers gingerly and placed them in cardboard boxes. Gwen put the columns and the little bride and groom figures in a paper bag and wished us luck.

The first twelve miles of our trip went smoothly because we were on major highways. We turned on to the winding country road we had to follow for the last eight miles and Libby gasped and grabbed my arm. "Look out for that pothole!" I swerved and the boxes in the backseat went sliding to one side. We hugged a blind curve and they slid back to the other side. We went over a bump and they leapt like three Mexican jumping beans. We hit a stretch where the road surface was rippled like a giant washboard; the boxes jiggled like Jell-O. Libby kept turning around and giving them looks of dismay. "How did you end up having to do this?" she asked me.

"I guess Medwin hadn't thought about how the cake was going to get there. He's not a master of logistics. We'll probably arrive and discover I'm the best man."

We pulled up in front of the Bales place. A tiny handful of people were milling around the yard. We carried the three boxes over the wooden footbridge that led to the house and went up on the porch. "Cake delivery!" I called out. Medwin and Lucy came to the door and stared at the boxes. They were expecting a fully assembled architectural wonder of a cake, and this wasn't it.

"This is Libby," I introduced her.

"Hi, nice to meet you," she said. "We need a table."

They led us inside to the kitchen table. Libby told the young bride and groom that it was bad luck for them to see the wedding cake before they were married, and she shooed them out of the kitchen. I held my breath as she opened the first box. To our great relief the bottom tier had arrived intact, with all the piping and curlicues and roses where they were supposed to be. We lifted the cake carefully out of the box and put it in the middle of the table. "Even if the other sections didn't make it we have one good part," Libby celebrated. She opened the box that contained the middle tier. "It's not too bad," she assessed it. "I can cover the bald spots with icing." I was sure the top tier was going to be a train wreck, but it wasn't any worse than the second.

We puzzled over the miracle of the cake. "How could it take such a beating and still look like this?" Libby wondered.

"Gwen used Super Glue in the icing," I speculated.

Medwin's mother came in. "Mrs. Bales, this is my fiancée Libby," I introduced them.

"I don't even know who *you* are," she reacted.

"Greg Johnson," I refreshed her memory. "I drove Medwin to Institute."

"Oh, yeah."

A girl of about ten appeared. "What are you doing?" she asked us.

"Putting all the parts of the cake together," Libby explained. "What's your name?"

"Marcie. My brother's getting married."

"I bet you're pretty excited."

"I'm getting his bedroom," Marcie kept it in perspective.

"Mrs. Bales, would you help me with this cake?" Libby requested.

"I'll do it," Marcie volunteered.

I took this as my cue to exit. The crowd outside had swelled to about twenty people. I was surprised to see that one of them was my neighbor, Yvonne Standard. She was wearing clerical garb. "Hi Yvonne."

She flashed a broad smile. "Well, what are you doing here, Greg??"

"I was going to ask you the same thing. How do you know Medwin and Lucy?"

"They came to my church last week and asked me to marry them. I think the other ministers turned them down. The way I look at it, if these two children want to get married, God bless 'em. I know they have problems, but if folks with problems couldn't get married there wouldn't be any weddings."

"I know Medwin through my work," I explained. "He's not my client but I've helped him out a couple of times."

She looked around and lowered her voice to a whisper. "He told me he was born on a roller coaster. Can you imagine a mother like that?"

"I wouldn't put a lot of stock in that story, Yvonne. I don't think they let you on roller coasters when you're nine months pregnant. But Mrs. Bales is different. She doesn't seem to be helping with the wedding. Medwin made the invitations himself and handed them out yesterday. He asked me to pick up the wedding cake. Libby and I just delivered it."

"Is Libby here? I love that girl! You know our whole family's coming to your wedding. We wouldn't miss it."

"Ours is outdoors, too. Just pray it doesn't rain. I understand you have some pull with the Weather Man."

"I'll pray for sunshine and 75 degrees," she promised.

Jack McManus arrived and got out of his car. He'd lost some weight, but he looked good. "How's the heart patient?" I asked him.

"Rumors of my demise have been greatly exaggerated," he quoted Mark Twain. "I tried to get you on the phone this morning. I want to ask you something." He made his way across the bridge and looked around to make sure no one was listening to us. "Do you want your Jeep decorated?"

"What do you mean?"

"Medwin didn't ask you?"

"About what?"

"Rosalee Detch is giving them a free room for the night at the Fort Savannah Inn. They're planning to ride back to town with you. Medwin asked me to bring some shaving cream and shoe polish and tin cans and balloons to decorate your Jeep. He's picturing a grand entrance into town. I told him to ask you about it."

"He hasn't mentioned it."

"What do you want me to do with all this stuff?"

"Please keep it in your car. I really don't want mine messed up."

"What if he asks me about it? I can't very well turn him down on his wedding day. These kids need something to remember."

"Jack, please don't. Try to talk him out of it."

"Medwin's stubborn. You know how he gets fixated on things."

"Okay, bottom line: the shaving cream and balloons are okay, but the tin cans and shoe polish are out."

He gave me a thumbs-up. "Got it."

I thought the best strategy was to hide my vehicle somewhere. But the Bales family lived on a road that wound along a creek, and all the houses were highly visible. Unless I wanted to drive two miles up the road, ditch it in the woods and walk back, there weren't any hiding places. Even if I chose that course of action, it would take me forty minutes to get back to the wedding. I made a mental note for my own wedding day: stash the getaway car.

Libby and Marcie carried a card table into the yard and brought out the cake, which had been restored to its original glory. The ceremony started, with all of us standing. The bride and groom were wearing their regular clothes because they didn't have anything better. The attendees were their neighbors. Yvonne did her best to lend an air of formality to the simple affair. Lucy didn't have anyone to give her away, so Yvonne improvised and had all of us give her away, even though it didn't make much sense. It was a bittersweet occasion, with Medwin and Lucy going through the motions but just missing the mark.

The wedding cake was the one grand touch. In the process of restoring it Libby had inherited the job of serving, which meant disassembling it again. She cut the cake into generous pieces and dispatched Marcie to deliver them to the guests on paper towels – no one had thought to get plastic plates, forks or napkins, so we nibbled on it picnic-style. The reception wound down quickly, with people congratulating the newlyweds, who could only think to say, "Thanks," in reply.

As we were climbing into my decorated vehicle, Mrs. Bales came over. "Where are the tin cans?" she inquired.

"I don't want tin cans," I replied. "They make too much noise. We have to drive 20 miles."

"You've got to have them," she informed me. "They're good luck. They scare away the evil spirits."

I started to argue with her and I thought better of it. I called to Jack, "Tie on one of those strings of tin cans."

While he was taking care this, Mrs. Bales had some advice for her son. "Make sure you carry her over the threshold, Medwin. If she trips you'll have bad luck. You'll end up getting divorced."

As his mother walked away Medwin gave me a puzzled look. "What's a threshold?"

"It means you carry her into the motel room instead of letting her walk in herself."

Libby looked at me; I don't think she'd thought about this before. "Are you planning to carry me over the threshold?"

"No," I said. "If we both ended up with broken arms it would be bad luck, too."

When we were a mile or so down the road I stopped and yanked off the string of cans. "Why'd you do that?" Medwin complained.

"I'm pretty sure we've warded off all the evil spirits, Medwin. We've got a long ride. Here's a souvenir." I gave him the cans and we went on our way. I'd traveled many country roads in my first year as a social worker, but never with the faces of a bride and groom staring back from the rearview mirror. Libby was proving to be a good sport when it came to my job. She'd quickly accepted that these quirky little episodes were going to happen, and she went with the flow.

When we reached the city limits Medwin and Lucy sat up straighter. "Honk!" he said excitedly. "Everybody here knows me!"

I wasn't wild about making a grand entrance, like Jesus into Jerusalem. "Everybody here knows me, too, Medwin," I let him know. Libby gave me a quick look, and I knew it meant I was supposed to honk to make them happy. We rode downtown with the newlyweds waving like they were a royal couple. People honked and waved and yelled their congratulations. I realized it was probably the high point of their wedding day, so I pulled over to the side of the road and tied the string of tin cans back on the rear bumper. We pulled up to the Fort Savannah Inn making as much noise as we could make without getting arrested.

We dropped them off, wished them luck and headed back to Alderson. The Carpenters' song *We've Only Just Begun* came on the radio and Libby smiled. "That's very appropriate," she said. "For them and for us."

An hour before our wedding Libby was sitting on her parents' front porch in shorts, chatting with friends and looking relaxed. It wasn't traditional for the groom to see the bride before the wedding ceremony, but we'd long ago abandoned tradition. We wanted a day that reflected us, not a ritual where we were cast in roles, delivering our lines like we were following a script. We'd written the ceremony ourselves after researching what had to be included to make it legal. As we'd originally envisioned, we were getting married under a dogwood tree in the backyard. Dave Sweet, one of my Concord social work students who was a gifted musician, had put together a bluegrass band to provide the music for the occasion. In place of *The Wedding March*, Libby walked in to the strains of the Carter Family's song *You Are My Flower*.

You are my flower
That's blooming in the mountain so high
You are my flower
That's blooming there for me

When summertime is gone and snow begins to fall
You can sing this song and say to one and all
You are my flower
That's blooming in the mountain so high
You are my flower
That's blooming there for me

So wear a happy smile and life will be worthwhile

Forget the tears but don't forget to smile
You are my flower
That's blooming in the mountain so high
You are my flower
That's blooming there for me

We included a couple of lines about sharing our lives in a home filled with music and books. One of our friends read Chapter 13 of Paul's *First Letter to the Corinthians*, and another one read the lyrics to Bob Dylan's song *Forever Young*. Nearly 300 people were in attendance. The Alderson Volunteer Fire Department had borrowed chairs from the elementary school cafeteria and set them up.

During the planning process we had encountered a bit of a problem. Libby's side of the family included some teetotaler aunts, conservative types who would have frowned if alcohol were served at the reception. My side of the family and our friends wouldn't have considered it a wedding if the drinks weren't flowing freely. Once again Anne Blair saved the day. "We'll have a party at my house for Greg's family and your friends," she proposed. "I just bought a new turkey smoker. I need an excuse to try it out."

So on our wedding day we had two receptions, one very dry and one very wet. The second one at Anne Blair's stately Victorian home on Washington Street went on late into the night. We made a discovery: everyone who comes to a wedding wants some face time with the newlyweds. We're both extroverts and we loved the chance to catch up with relatives and friends from near and far, but we left the first reception having eaten only the token bites of wedding cake we'd fed each other, mainly for the benefit of the photographer. We were expecting to chow down at Anne Blair's, but enthusiastic revelers offering their congratulations inundated us. The smoked turkey smelled mouth-watering, but we never tasted it, or any of the food served in our honor that day. Fueled only by the glasses of champagne people kept putting in our hands, we said our goodbyes and headed off to Warm Springs, Virginia, where we were spending the first night of our honeymoon.

As we were pulling out of Anne Blair's driveway my cousin Meg came running up. "Wait!" she yelled. "I've got a joke to tell you."

"Okay," I said. "But it better be good."

"A young, innocent couple got married," she launched into her story. "After the wedding they went to the motel where they were spending the night. They'd never seen each other naked before. The groom started to undress and when he took off his socks the bride saw that his toes were twisted and deformed. 'Oh, my gosh,' she reacted. 'What happened to your toes?'

'When I was a little boy I had tolio,' he explained.

'Tolio? I've never heard of tolio.'

'Well I had it,' he insisted.

He resumed undressing. When he took off his pants his new wife was surprised to see that his knees were gnarled and mangled. 'What happened to your knees?'

'When I was young I had the kneasles,' he told her.

'The kneasles?'

He nodded. 'Once you have them you never get them again.'

When he took off his underwear she gasped. 'Oh, my God! You had smallcox, too!' "

Smirking and looking very proud of herself, she wished us luck and waved goodbye.

"Thanks, Meg," I said. "On our Silver Anniversary, even if we don't remember anything else about our wedding day, we'll remember your stupid joke."

We left our friends and family still partying in Anne Blair's backyard and crossed the state border to Virginia on I-64. As we took the Covington exit to go to Warm Springs, we spotted a Hardee's sign. "I'm starving," I said.

"I am, too," Libby agreed.

So on our wedding night, after spending six hours at two receptions in our honor with scrumptious food we never sampled, we drove through Hardee's, ordered two cheeseburgers and headed off to whatever the future held in store for us.

We'd only just begun, but it was already obvious that some days we were just going to have to improvise.

Afterword

Some social workers and counselors who read this book will undoubtedly question the way I handled particular situations, or if it's ethical to write about clients when there was a promise of confidentiality.

I find much of the literature related to my profession either too dry or too sentimental. I wanted to share my experiences in a more entertaining, less maudlin way. I decided to focus on stories from my early days as a young social worker, realizing that as a rookie I didn't always make the best choices.

I've used the real names of my family members and some friends. I've used the real names and personalities of former co-workers who are deceased, but replaced those who are living with fictional characters who aren't those people.

I've gone to lengths to protect my clients, changing whatever was necessary to make sure they can't be identified. All of the stories in *A Very Famous Social Worker* are based on actual experiences, but they've been doctored to whatever degree was necessary to preserve confidentiality. Because of this, the book walks a thin line between nonfiction and fiction.

Social work is a sometimes exhausting, always eye-opening pursuit, but caring for other people will never go out of style. As Mark Twain once observed, "Kindness is the language that the deaf can hear and the blind can see." Under the guiding hand of the late

Anne Blair Alderson, the Greenbrier Valley Mental Health Clinic was an exceptionally kind place, and I'm glad that as a young social worker I stumbled in the door and was taken into the family.